GOOD HOUSEKEEPING

Your

5

Ingredient
Dinner Plan

70+ RECIPES
for super-simple
meals every night
of the week

Contents

Recipes

Seared Chicken
with Cheesy Spinach
and Artichokes
(p.64)

Introduction

IF YOU WOULD love to enjoy a delicious, healthy, home-cooked meal most nights of the week, this cookbook is for you! And if planning, shopping for and making those meals feels overwhelming and nearly impossible to add to your crowded to-do list, this cookbook is also for you! The best part? The strategies we share don't require you to shop for a month's worth of food or set aside a whole day to prep a mountain of vegetables for the week.

Instead, this cookbook offers a refreshingly simple solution designed to reduce meal-time stress in a number of ways: First, the dinners only require a handful of ingredients—just five or less. Plus, by simply shrinking your shopping list, you increase the chances that you will actually use everything you buy (read: no more tossed produce or dollars wasted). And let's face it—life is just easier when you don't have to haul so many groceries home each week. Second, most of the recipes in this book can be whipped up with less than 30 minutes hands-on time.

To illustrate how this 5-ingredient formula can result in satisfying meals with BIG flavor that come together quickly, we created a 10-week dinner meal plan for you featuring 70 easy-to-prepare recipes—and we think you'll be impressed with the results. For example, imagine whipping up *Pan-Fried Chicken with Lemony Roasted Broccoli* (p.46) in 35 minutes, or enjoying the surprisingly delicious pairing of sweet and savory ingredients when you serve *Roasted Sausage and Grapes with Polenta* (p.166), which is ready in only 25 minutes! Of course, you don't have to restrict yourself to this minimalist approach as a hard-and-fast rule—if you're tempted to add something else to your dish, we say, "go for it!"

If this way of feeding your family sounds tricky, immerse yourself in the first two chapters. There, we'll fill you in on the best shopping and kitchen advice from the trusted experts in the The Good Housekeeping Test Kitchen, then we'll get into the nuts and bolts of how to create recipes based on what you have on hand and a customized meal plan that works for you.

With a reliable game plan in place, you can build easy, delicious and healthy dinners with only five main ingredients and schedule them for the weeks ahead. Plus, you'll save a considerable amount of money while spending less time in the kitchen and more time around the table with your loved ones. Let's get started!

From the Editors of *Good Housekeeping*

CHAPTER 1

Good Food
BASICS

Your Guide to Great Ingredients

NAVIGATING A MODERN grocery store, which on average is packed with over 30,000 items, can feel overwhelming for even the most experienced shopper. And, when you're taking a minimal approach of using five ingredients or less, the quality of your ingredients matter more than ever. But, once you know what to look for (and what to skip), it can become far easier. To help you make the best selections, experts in the Good Housekeeping Test Kitchen put together what you need to know about choosing the best staple ingredients that are both family-friendly and versatile.

PRODUCE

When shopping for fresh produce in a well-stocked grocery store, you can usually find almost anything. However, get in the habit of choosing items that are in season; they tend to be more affordable and will likely offer peak nutritional value and optimal flavor.

In the spring, try asparagus, broccoli, kale and pineapple. In the summer, opt for berries, watermelon, tomatoes, peaches and plums. In the fall, try apples, grapes, kiwi, collard greens and spinach. In the winter, consider parsnips, carrots, leeks, pumpkin and other winter squash.

MEAT AND SEAFOOD

When choosing meat, make sure that it is firm and dry, it should never look slimy or sticky and it should be cold to the touch. If it is already packaged, check that the packaging is free of holes or tears and check the date. If it is just a couple of days before the sell-by date, plan to cook it within the first day or two of purchasing it. For steaks and chops, look for meat that has been cut evenly and has similar thickness so each piece cooks at the same rate. This even size rule also applies to chicken breasts and thighs.

For fish and seafood, keep sustainability top of mind while shopping. The Monterey Bay Aquarium Seafood Watch (seafoodwatch.org) offers more guidance on the best types and cuts to buy.

DAIRY AND DAIRY ALTERNATIVES

When buying yogurt, especially flavored varieties, check the added sugar content. Aim for 8 grams (the equivalent of 2 teaspoons) or fewer per serving. Greek yogurt and skyr typically have higher protein counts.

If you're choosing a milk alternative, look at the ingredient list as well as the nutrition facts label to check the protein and added sugar content. Most milk alternatives have added sugar and little to no protein, so don't assume that all are nutritionally equivalent to milk. Alternatives made from soy and pea typically offer higher protein counts in the plant-based category.

FROZEN FOODS

Always be sure to check the ingredient list on frozen food, as many options have hidden sources of sodium, added sugar and saturated fat. Try to avoid breaded and fried foods as well as frozen meals that are high in sodium.

When shopping for frozen veggies, look for plain options without added salt, then season them yourself instead. For frozen fruit, look for unsweetened varieties with only 100% frozen fruit in the ingredient list.

Frozen grains are very easy to prepare: They take a fraction of the time to reheat compared to cooking dry grains and make for a great side dish at practically any meal.

BREADS, GRAINS AND CEREAL

For bread, don't assume that darker varieties are necessarily healthier. Some brands will add food coloring or molasses to make the bread appear an earthier color. Instead, look for options that say "100% Whole Wheat," "100% Whole Grain" or "100% Sprouted Grain." The same thing applies to English muffins and pita.

Granola can make a great snack, yogurt parfait topping or an added crunch to your favorite salads, but many brands in the supermarket are packed with added sugar. Make sure the first ingredient in the granola you choose is a whole grain or whole food (i.e., oats, nuts, bran, legumes, etc.). Try to choose options with at least 2 grams of fiber and protein per serving and less than 10 grams of added sugar per serving.

CANNED AND DRY GOODS

Take special care to look at the ingredient list and nutrition facts label for canned items, especially the sodium counts. If salt intake is something you are watching, try to choose varieties that are marked "Low-Sodium," "Reduced Sodium" or "No Added Salt."

Avoid extra added sugar by choosing fruits that are canned in water instead of juice or syrup. Ideally, look for cans that have BPA-free linings. Opt for raw, roasted or lightly salted varieties for nuts. For nut butters, always review the ingredient list: You should see nuts and maybe a little salt listed but nothing else. Avoid nut butters with added syrups and sugar sources.

CONDIMENTS

Because condiments offer a high-impact burst of flavor, using them wisely can be a delicious and simple way to prepare satisfying meals with fewer ingredients. But many store-bought options can be high in sugar, salt, calories and additives. Be sure to take a look at the ingredient list and also note the serving size.

Investing in a variety of spices and spice mixes is also a good way to add both flavor and aroma to dishes without extra salt or sugar. However, be mindful to use them before their "best by" date for optimal flavor, potency and color.

Oil and Vinegar
Chicken Cutlet
Sandwiches (p.80)

Let's Get Cooking

READY TO GET STARTED? Here is some basic cooking advice that's good to keep in mind.

USING THE RIGHT APPLIANCE FOR THE JOB

In the Good Housekeeping Institute Kitchen Appliances and Innovation Lab, we test a variety of kitchen equipment every day to find the best tools to make your work in the kitchen easier. We've included a roundup here of some of our favorite items.

AIR FRYER

This epic countertop appliance is unbelievably versatile and lends itself well to anything that requires a crispy, crunchy coating without a lot of added fat. It is essentially a mini-convection oven, which means it has a built-in fan to circulate hot air around your food as it cooks. Plus, with so much less oil used during cooking, cleanup is a breeze. Once you try our Air Fryer Fish and Chips (p.94), you may never want to use a deep fryer again.

OVEN

Baking and roasting in a traditional oven sometimes gets a bad rap because the perception is that it takes longer. However, the popularity of "sheet-pan meals" clearly demonstrates that with the right recipe, you can go from prep to plating in about 30 minutes. Looking for something different? Try our Shakshuka (p.90), which is ready in a flash and perfect for a busy weeknight. Who doesn't love breakfast for dinner?

GRILL

Whether you have an outdoor grill or an oven range with a grill feature, a good grill can deliver a dish full of intense flavor, thanks to its rapid and thorough browning capabilities. A grill is a natural cooking match for tender cuts of meat like chicken and steak. Give it a shot with our Grilled Pork with Smoky Corn Salad (p.128).

PRESSURE COOKER

Using a pressure cooker is one of the best hands-off ways to get dinner on the table quickly — one-pot meals like soups and stews come together faster than they do in the oven or on the stove using a Dutch oven. Pressure cookers also make it easy to work with budget-friendly cuts, like pork shoulder, which usually require hours of braising. They're great for busy cooks since you can have a full meal on the table in under an hour with minimal prep work. In most cases, you simply add ingredients to the pot with some liquid and cover it with the locking lid. And electric pressure cookers, such as the Instant Pot, make this method of cooking extra simple. Just try our Multicooker Coconut Beef Curry (p.36) and you'll see what we mean.

SAUTÉ PAN

A classic for a reason, sautéing is speedy and produces flavorful results. Cooking in a high-sided skillet with high heat and a tiny amount of oil yields quick dinners that come with their own pan sauces. Try it tonight with our Seared Pork Chops with Cherries and Spinach (p.98).

If you don't have one of these appliances in your kitchen already, check out our website before buying one to see what brands we recommend.

Stretch Your Food Dollars: Our Best Advice for Shopping on a Budget

Even with grocery prices on the rise, there are still plenty of ways to save both time and money if you're concerned about keeping your costs low. Consider the following:

TRY SHOPPING MIDWEEK.

If your schedule permits, avoid weekend shopping trips whenever possible. Deals tend to be better in the middle of the week when grocery stores restock their shelves and mark down what didn't sell from the week before.

PRACTICE "FIRST IN, FIRST OUT."

As you unpack your groceries, move older products to the front of the fridge/freezer/pantry, and put new products in the back. This way, you're more likely to use up the older foods before they spoil (which saves money and reduces waste!).

BROWSE ALL LEVELS OF SHELVING.

Store shelf placement matters, and you may be paying a premium for items that are set at eye level; they tend to be the most expensive options. Look at the higher and lower shelves for better prices, with many generic options being stocked on the lower shelves.

ALWAYS USE A LIST.

You'll find a shopping list for every weekly menu in this book, but it's still a good idea to stick to a well-defined list for all the other household items you might need during the week. Remember to check your pantry to avoid buying what you already have on hand. Once you get to the store, having a list makes it far easier to reduce impulse buys and stick to what you really need.

BE STRATEGIC ABOUT BULK SHOPPING.

Buying in bulk can give you a better price per unit — but only if you actually use all of what you buy. While it may be tempting to stock up, consider how quickly you might consume the great deal in front of you, whether some of it can be easily frozen for future use, and make sure to check expiration dates so nothing will go to waste.

CONSIDER A REBATE OR LOYALTY APP.

Services like *Ibotta* provide free cash-back rewards for a huge number of grocery retailers. You can scan the barcodes at the store to find out if there are any rebates available, or just save your receipt and upload an image to the app to get cash back. If you frequent the same grocery store every week, it's worth finding out whether or not the store offers a loyalty card or app with rewards and coupons. It's in a store's best interest to keep you coming back, so many will offer loyal customers exclusive discounts on popular items.

The Wonders of Meal Prepping

WHILE THIS BOOK is all about meal planning, it's worth discussing how meal prepping can save you time on busy weeknights (and money on your grocery bill!) by making sure you have ready-to-go ingredients when you need them. It's completely optional. But if you have a few minutes here or there, meal prepping can really put you ahead. Some people prefer to do all their prep on a Sunday. Others like to split the work between Sunday and Wednesday, which allows for flexibility should you end up craving something specific mid-week. Here are the strategies that can make meal prepping easier:

1. PREP INGREDIENTS

Prepping can include chopping, peeling, slicing or roasting ingredients in advance, or putting together the ingredients for a multistep dish to cook later. If you're new to meal prepping, you might want to start with prep for two to three days' worth of meals.

2. PORTION BULK ITEMS

Divvy up large containers of yogurt, applesauce, nuts, etc., into portions — enough for use in a meal for four, for example. You can also pack away portions from your big-batch cooking (see right) into individual servings ahead of time if you're planning to grab the food for lunch or breakfast.

3. COOK BIG BATCHES

Make large multi-serving recipes — or double your favorite recipes — and store them for use later in the week or freeze them for up to three months. Cooking a big pot of beans or a double batch of rice, or preparing a large piece of meat to use across several meals can also cut down on day-of prep. Of course, what qualifies as "big-batch" to you will depend on the number of people in your household, the size of their appetites and the amount of fridge and freezer space you have.

Cooking Secrets Chefs Swear By

SET YOURSELF UP for success and make your time in the kitchen as efficient as possible with these recommendations from the pros.

MASTER MISE EN PLACE.

This might be the most important tip of all. "Mise en place" is French for "everything in place." What does it mean to a chef? Before you start cooking, have your ingredients peeled, chopped and measured, and pans greased and within reach, etc. This will keep you from running around looking for the dried basil while your sauce is on the brink of burning.

PUT A WET PAPER TOWEL UNDER A CUTTING BOARD.

Not only are cutting boards that slide on the counter annoying, they're extremely dangerous when you're holding a knife and trying to chop something. Wet a paper towel and lay it under the board and it won't budge!

KEEP PIECES UNIFORM.

Ever wonder why chefs spend so much time learning how to chop vegetables into similar-size pieces? It's the best way to make sure they cook at the same rate. If your ingredient size varies widely, you may find elements of your finished dish both under- and overcooked, so strive for consistency with your chopping skills.

DON'T CROWD THE SKILLET.

When roasting or browning anything, the tendency is to cram as much in the pan as possible. Resist! Use a larger pan or cook in smaller batches instead. Crowding the pan leads to steaming and lowers the temperature of the pan so you won't get the caramelization you're looking for — and that's where the flavor is.

CONSIDER TONGS AN EXTENSION OF YOUR HAND.

Walk into any restaurant kitchen and you'll see a set of tongs in almost every cook's hand — usually gripped low down on the handle for maximum control. Use it to flip meat, pull a pan out of the oven, stabilize a steak while slicing — the list goes on and on.

USE YOUR SENSES.

If something in the oven smells done but the timer's still ticking, check on it. Recipes offer valuable guidelines for best results and the Good Housekeeping Test Kitchen strives to ensure your success in the kitchen every time, but equipment and ingredients can vary from kitchen to kitchen, so don't forget that the most important factor in a dish coming out the way you want it is YOU!

FOOD STORAGE 101

In the Good Housekeeping Institute Kitchen Appliances and Innovation Lab, we test a variety of kitchen equipment every day to find the best tools to make your work in the kitchen easier. We've included a roundup here of some of our favorite items.

PICK THE RIGHT CONTAINERS.

Always make sure to let cooked food cool down before packing it away (putting hot food in the fridge or freezer is a no-no). Then select your containers. You can use plastic or glass containers (as long as they are freezer-safe and have airtight lids) or even resealable plastic or silicone freezer bags. Stackable square or rectangular containers will maximize fridge space. Quart-size mason jars are great for soups and stews.

PORTION WISELY.

It's helpful to divide your food into portion sizes that will feed your household, so you can grab the exact amount you need when it's time to cook. Individual pieces of food (chicken breasts, hamburger patties, slices of pizza, etc.) can be wrapped tightly in plastic wrap and then in aluminum foil before going in the fridge or freezer. Ladle big-batch soups, stews and tomato sauces into quart-size containers that are easy to thaw.

LABEL YOUR CONTAINERS.

Here's a chef tip that's easy to adapt for home use: With a Sharpie, write the name of the dish and the date on a piece of masking tape, then affix the tape to your container before you put it in the fridge or freezer.

PLAY IT SAFE.

Prepared foods can remain refrigerated for 2 to 5 days or frozen for 3 to 4 months, depending on the ingredients — ground meat and raw sausage can be stored in the freezer for up to 4 months, bacon, chicken and chops can go for up to 6 months, steaks, hot dogs and fully cooked sausage can go for up to 8 months, and chicken parts can go for up to 9 months. To play it safe and avoid foodborne illness, keep food out of the "danger zone" — temperatures between 40°F and 140°F. Sealing food in airtight packaging or storage containers will not only keep bacteria out, but also protect the flavor and lock moisture in.

Ham and Brie
Quesadillas
(p.104)

CHAPTER 2

Your Recipe for Success:
MEAL PLANS MADE EASY

What is a Meal Plan?

AT ITS CORE, a meal plan is a group of recipes you have committed to making over a specific time period (like a week). There are plenty of reasons to use a meal plan: to save money, eat healthier and to make mealtimes less stressful. Once you have that list, you can purchase ingredients you need in advance, so when mealtime approaches, you can start cooking with intention (a.k.a. not scrambling to assess the fridge or throwing things together in a panic). A great meal plan will offer variety, enticing flavor combinations and convenience—which for most of us means not a lot of pots and pans and getting food on the table in a limited amount of time. The chapter ahead will show you how to put together a meal plan that works for you, as well as provide tips if you decide to follow a premade plan like the one we share in Chapter 3.

Potato and Chorizo Tacos (p.40)

Getting Started

THE KEY TO a good meal plan is setting aside a little time to really think about how to maximize your effort in the kitchen. Follow these steps to make getting dinner on the table easy every day of the week.

FIGURE OUT YOUR SCHEDULE.
Start by sitting down and looking at your calendar for the next week. Note which days you have plans for eating out, or which weeknights might be particularly busy and will need a quick and easy dinner. Next, if you prefer to get some of the work done ahead of time, pick a day (or two) to do your meal prepping (see The Wonders of Meal Prepping, p.13). Using this existing schedule, you can start plotting out what you'd like to eat each day.

THINK ABOUT WHO YOU'RE COOKING FOR.
Whether feeding a pasta-loving family, making dinners just for two, or working toward your own personal

health goal that calls for low-carb meals, knowing who you're making meals for helps narrow down the kinds of dishes you will want to cook.

ASSESS YOUR PANTRY AND FRIDGE.

Take a look at what you have on hand and see if you can make meals from—or at least include—those canned goods and frozen foods you already have stocked. Knowing exactly what's in your pantry and fridge will also help you avoid buying duplicates, so consider making an inventory list if you find that helpful.

LEAN INTO VARIETY.

By nature, successful meal planning means you won't eat the same thing every day. This is possible even if you find yourself gravitating to a particular protein (those large value packs of boneless skinless chicken breasts are hard to beat when you find a good sale), thanks to the endless number of sides and sauces at your disposal. Imagine your favorite dishes at restaurants you frequent and take inspiration from their combinations. Give steamed cod a Chinese-inspired touch by pairing it with some garlicky bok choy one day, then bake it the next day with some onions, mini sweet peppers, grape tomatoes, fresh thyme and some olive oil for a taste of the Mediterranean. The possibilities are endless.

MAXIMIZE INGREDIENTS.

Once you start planning your meals, you'll have an opportunity to take leftover ingredients to a new level. When making your grocery list, note the items that come in larger quantities than you need and think ahead to other uses for them. For example, if the chimichurri sauce you are serving with your steak calls for only a few tablespoons of parsley, you could spin the leftover herbs into a quick omelet the next day.

GET CREATIVE.

If you're missing an ingredient—or just crave a different flavor profile—feel free to swap in a simple substitution (instead of running out to the store). Just make sure you stick with ingredients similar to what the recipe calls for, so replace one soft herb with another, one variety of canned beans with another or a splash of oil with a different type of fat. Have fun mixing and matching sauces, sides, grains and proteins. Find flavors you love and textures you enjoy while building your menu rotation.

Sheet Pan Asparagus Frittata (p.102)

Make Your Own Meal Plan

ONCE YOU'VE IDENTIFIED which nights you want to cook and the ingredients you have on hand, it's time to decide what dishes to make. Using the grid on p.21 will give you a jump start on planning your meals. Because dinner is often the biggest hurdle, we've listed it first on the grid, with lunch, breakfast and snack following. You can base the meals on dishes you know or like to riff on—for inspiration, you'll find information on basic cooking techniques and key ingredients that can do double duty later in this chapter. Or you can opt for more standard recipes (go to goodhousekeeping.com/recipe to find hundreds of dinner ideas). Fill out the sections for protein, flavor, cooking method and sides using the guidelines just below. Then jot down which key ingredients you already have on hand and what you'll need to get at the grocery.

Here are some factors to consider when making a dinner menu:

PLAN AROUND YOUR FAVORITE PROTEINS.

Whether you choose meat or seafood (or prefer to stick to a plant-based option), your protein is usually the centerpiece of any dish. Cook what you love. But also make a point to experiment now and then with proteins you aren't too familiar with. You may just find another gem to add to your rotation.

IDENTIFY A FLAVOR PROFILE.

While the phrase "flavor profile" might sound intimidating, it's really just a way to make sure the ingredients you choose complement one another. Another way to approach this challenge is to consider the seasonings common in a particular cuisine. Think soy, sesame and ginger for Chinese dishes, oregano and basil for a taste of Italy, or a combination of fish sauce, lime juice and bird chiles for a Thai kick.

DETERMINE YOUR COOKING METHOD.

If you cook enough meals, you'll find there are usually several ways to prepare any given dish. If you're not planning to follow a specific recipe, it's a very good idea to think about what cooking method will work best for you on any given night. Are you too busy to watch a pan as your food cooks? A slow cooker or air fryer might be your best option. Does the weather report look promising for a particular evening? It could be the perfect time to fire up the grill and enjoy a meal al fresco.

ROUND OUT WITH SIDES.

Once you have your game plan for your main protein, make a point to consider the sides that make your plate complete. Does your main dish already feature a vegetable or starchy component like noodles or rice? If so, that's one less ingredient to worry about adding to your plate. Consider a soup or garnishing with fresh herbs instead. The point is to think through your menu completely and commit to a strategy for each meal.

DON'T FORGET THE DETAILS.

If your dish includes working ahead or making double-batches, make sure to include any prep notes you'll want to remember.

USE THIS CHART TO GET A JUMP START ON PLANNING YOUR MEALS

	Sunday	Monday	Tuesday	Wednesday	Thursday	Friday	Saturday
Dinner Proteins							
Flavor							
Method							
Side							
Prep Notes							
Lunch							
Breakfast							
Snacks							

INGREDIENTS I HAVE:

PRODUCE:

PROTEIN:

DAIRY:

PANTRY:

GROCERY LIST:

PRODUCE:

PROTEIN:

DAIRY:

PANTRY:

Cook It Right

Good Housekeeping's secret to delicious steak, chops and chicken breasts? Repeat this mantra: "Set up, sear, roast." Follow these steps to get a beautiful brown crust and the center cooked through just right.

SET UP

Pat the meat dry (extra moisture causes it to steam rather than sear) and let it sit at room temperature for 20 minutes.

Heat the oven to 400°F. Heat a 12-inch skillet on medium-high (for the best crust, don't use nonstick). Season the meat evenly on both sides with salt and pepper, being extra generous with red meat.

SEAR

Add 1 Tbsp olive oil to the hot skillet and swirl it to evenly coat the bottom of the pan. Add the meat and sear until the bottom is nicely browned.

Carefully flip the meat and sear until the other side is browned too. Rotate the skillet to ensure even browning.

ROAST

Transfer the meat to a small rimmed baking sheet in a single layer (don't rinse the skillet just yet!) and roast to desired doneness or, for chicken, until cooked through.

Transfer the meat to a cutting board and let it rest for at least half its total cooking time to help it stay juicy and make it easier to slice. Don't forget to save any extra juices for the pan sauce.

TOP IT OFF

Don't put your pan in the sink just yet! After searing the meat, you can use the drippings in your skillet to make a deliciously flavorful (and simple!) sauce.

1. Immediately after transferring your meat to the oven, start your sauce: Turn the heat to low. There should be about 2 Tbsp of fat in the pan. (In a 12-inch skillet, that's a thin, even coating on the bottom. If there's more, pour a little off. If there's less, add some olive oil.)

2. Add some chopped alliums (onions, shallots, leeks, scallions, garlic, etc.) and cook, stirring often, until slightly translucent and just tender, 2 to 3 minutes (do not let them brown).

3. Add ½ cup liquid (dry white or red wine or chicken broth) and simmer, stirring and scraping the bottom and sides of the pan to incorporate any stuck-on brown bits into the liquid. Stir in any juices from the roasting pan and cutting board and continue simmering until the mixture has reduced by about a third, 2 to 3 minutes (this is enough time for any alcohol to burn off).

4. For a creamy sauce, stir in a splash of heavy cream and simmer another minute or two until slightly thickened or remove from heat and swirl in a tablespoon of cold butter.

5. Taste the sauce, then season with additional salt and pepper, if needed. If desired, scatter chopped fresh herbs over the warm sauce just before serving.

Perfect Roasted Vegetables, Every Time.

Vegetables benefit from the high dry heat of the oven. Their flavor becomes concentrated and their natural sugars caramelize, transforming them into richly satisfying sides.

For every 1 lb vegetables, prep and cut into evenly sized pieces, then toss with 1 to 2 Tbsp olive oil and season as desired. Spread in a single layer on a rimmed baking sheet, leaving space in between the pieces so they caramelize well. Roast at 450°F, stirring once or twice during cooking, until golden brown and tender. If you are roasting a large amount of vegetables to use in your meal prep, divide them between two baking sheets (overcrowding the vegetables will cause them to steam instead of roast). Rotate pans between upper and lower oven racks halfway through cooking. You can roast different vegetables together if their cooking times are similar. If you happen to have leftover roasted vegetables, turn them into filling, big-flavor toppings on build-your-own dishes like pizza, tacos and grain bowls.

DOUBLE DUTY INSPIRATION

Many sauces, dressings and marinades have multiple uses, so if you're trying to cook with fewer ingredients, it makes sense to incorporate them whenever you can. When planning your menu, consider these ideas or create your own!

VINAIGRETTE

Dress your leafy greens, plus:

- Repurpose as a marinade for chicken
- Use as a sauce on fish or grilled vegetables
- Toss with a pasta or grain salad for extra flavor

DRY RUBS

Spice up your grilled meat, plus:

- Stir 1 Tbsp dry rub into a bowl of cooked pinto beans
- Use to season popcorn or nuts
- Mix 2 Tbsp dry rub with a stick of softened butter to spread on bread or corn on the cob

PESTO

Stir into your pasta, plus:

- Drop a dollop onto grilled chicken or steak
- Spread on a sandwich in place of mayo or mustard
- Stir into yogurt or sour cream for a dip for veggies or chips

SALSA

Dip your chips, plus:

- Simmer on low and use as a base for poaching eggs
- Stir into mac and cheese
- Spoon on a cooked fillet of white fish

TOMATO SAUCE

Toss with your spaghetti, plus:

- Use for braising chicken or beef
- Stir into cooked white beans or cooked rice
- Top a warm bowl of sauce with polenta or risotto

Black Bean–
Stuffed Poblano
Peppers (p.52)

CHAPTER 3

Get a Jumpstart with our
5-INGREDIENT MENU PLAN

Meal Plan Elements

EACH MEAL HAS been developed and tested by the Good Housekeeping Test Kitchen to provide maximum flavor with minimal effort. To help you kick off your meal planning journey, we created a handy 5-Ingredient Menu Plan featuring 10 weeks of delicious dinners—a different one for every day of the week. We've grouped the 70 recipes by season—Weeks 1 and 2 feature recipes best made in the winter, Weeks 3 to 5 feature the best that spring has to offer, Weeks 6 to 8 are best enjoyed in the summer, and Weeks 9 and 10 feature all the comforts of fall—so you can make them when the ingredients are at their peak. Though substitutions are easy and the recipes are versatile enough to enjoy all year round.

Included in this collection you'll also find:

BONUS RECIPES

We know that sometimes you won't be able to find a smaller amount of an ingredient or it simply makes more sense to buy in bulk. So we peppered bonus recipes throughout the plan to level up your next-day breakfast or lunch. The more you get into the practice of maximizing your ingredients, the more likely it will be that everything you buy will end up on your table—not in the trash.

FLAVOR BOOSTERS

We added some simple ways to take these dishes to a whole new level, that typically call for an extra ingredient or two. These will be in bold as an added finishing touch to your dish, and are all optional. If you have the ingredients on hand, we highly recommend sprinkling them in. No worries if you don't—the recipes we share in this book are also great on their own!

TEST KITCHEN TIPS

The recipes in this book offer a variety of ways to make dinner, but we know that not everyone has an air fryer or a multicooker. For that reason, we included tips for how to make these meals in the oven or on a stovetop as well.

WEEKLY SHOPPING LISTS

Our comprehensive shopping lists ensure you have everything you need on hand in the correct quantities to make seven meals. The items are organized by food groups for more efficient grocery runs. Each weekly list also includes a section for cooking staples (your butter, oils, salt and pepper). These are not counted as part of the core five ingredients since you most likely already keep them in stock. If you choose to take advantage of the suggested flavor boosters, you can find these ingredients in the "Boost It" section of the weekly list. Snap a photo and reference it on your grocery run.

RECIPE FINDER

Done with the 10-week plan and ready to create your own meal plan? Check out the Recipe Finder section at the end of the book on p.188. Organized by main ingredients, it will help you choose recipes according to what you love or have on hand.

Most recipes in this meal plan are developed to serve 4 to 6 people. However, they can be eaten as leftovers if you're cooking for fewer people, doubled to cater to bigger parties, or even reinvented to make a completely new meal for lunch the next day.

WEEK 1 DINNERS
Week-At-A-Glance

DAY 1
Seared Salmon with
Charred Green Beans

DAY 2
Roasted Butternut Squash and
Pork Chops with Cider Pan Sauce

DAY 3
Moroccan-Spiced Skillet
Chicken and Couscous

DAY 4
Multicooker Coconut
Beef Curry

DAY 5
Tomato Soup with
Parmesan Crostini

DAY 6
Potato and Chorizo Tacos

DAY 7
Pasta e Piselli

NOTES

_____

_____

_____

_____

_____

WEEK 1
Shopping List

Buy just what you need each week. Below are exact amounts of every ingredient you will need for Week 1.

PRODUCE
2   heads garlic
2   red onions
1   white onion
1   yellow onion
1¼ lb russet potatoes
1   1¼ lb butternut squash
½   small red cabbage (about 12 oz)
2¾ lb tomatoes
1   lb green beans
1   small red chile

MEAT & SEAFOOD
2   lbs beef chuck roast
4   bone-in pork chops (about 2¼ lbs total)
4   6-oz boneless, skinless chicken breasts
1   lb fresh Mexican chorizo
4   5-oz skinless salmon fillets

REFRIGERATED & DAIRY
1   cup apple cider
1   3-oz Parmesan wedge (with rind)

FROZEN
1   cup frozen peas

BREAD & BAKERY
4   ½-in.-thick slices baguette
8   small corn tortillas

PANTRY
2   Tbsp capers
1   14.5-oz can coconut milk
2   cups ditalini pasta
1   cup quick-cooking pearl couscous
1   Tbsp ras el hanout
¼   preserved lemon
2   Tbsp tomato paste
3   Tbsp red curry paste
1   Tbsp reduced-sodium chicken bouillon base (we used Better than Bouillon)
½   cup salsa verde
1   Tbsp whole-grain mustard

COOKING STAPLES
1   8-oz bottle olive oil
    Kosher salt and black pepper

BOOST IT

Some recipes this week may call for these flavor boosters and we highly recommend sprinkling them in if you already have them on hand. If you don't, it's OK—all the recipes are great on their own!

- Lemon
- Fresh parsley
- Fresh cilantro
- Cooked white rice
- Lime
- Red chile

Seared Salmon with Charred Green Beans

ACTIVE **20 MIN.** | TOTAL **20 MIN.**

INGREDIENTS

SALMON
4 5-oz skinless fillets

GREEN BEANS
1 lb, trimmed

GARLIC
4 cloves

CAPERS
2 Tbsp, rinsed and
patted dry

RED CHILE
1 small chile,
thinly sliced

1. Heat **2 tsp olive oil** in a large skillet on medium-high. Season salmon fillets with **½ tsp each kosher salt and pepper**. Add to skillet, reduce heat to medium and cook until just opaque throughout, 5 to 6 min. per side.

2. Heat **2 Tbsp oil** in large cast-iron skillet on medium-high. Add green beans and cook until browned, 2 to 3 min. Turn with tongs and cook until browned and just barely tender, about 3 min. more.

3. Meanwhile, smash garlic, then thinly slice. Remove cast-iron pan from heat and toss beans with **¼ tsp salt**, then garlic.

4. Return to medium heat and add capers.

5. Stir in red chile and cook, tossing, until garlic is golden brown, 1 to 2 min. Serve with salmon, with **lemon wedges** if desired.

SERVES 4 *About 285 calories, 14.5 g fat (2.5 g sat), 31 g pro, 540 mg sodium, 9 g carb, 3 g fiber*

BONUS IDEA	**Leftover Lunch:** *Toss a handful of capers in egg salad and serve on thick slices of toasted or grilled bread as an open-faced sandwich.*

Roasted Butternut Squash and Pork Chops with Cider Pan Sauce

ACTIVE **25 MIN.** | TOTAL **40 MIN.**

INGREDIENTS

BUTTERNUT SQUASH
about 1¼ lbs, peeled, seeded and cut into ½-in.-thick wedges or half moons

RED CABBAGE
about 12 oz, cut into 1-in.-thick wedges

PORK CHOPS
4 small bone-in (2¼ lbs total)

APPLE CIDER
1 cup

WHOLE-GRAIN MUSTARD
1 Tbsp

1. Heat oven to 450°F. Toss butternut squash and red cabbage, with **2 Tbsp olive oil** and ¼ tsp each kosher salt and pepper on a large rimmed baking sheet. Roast until golden brown on bottom and tender, 25 to 30 min.

2. Meanwhile, heat a large cast-iron skillet on medium. Season pork chops with **½ tsp each salt and pepper**. Add **1 Tbsp oil** to skillet and cook pork chops until golden brown and just cooked through, 6 to 8 min. per side; transfer to plate.

3. Pour off and discard any fat in skillet. Add apple cider, whole-grain mustard and any pork juices on plate and vigorously simmer, stirring occasionally, until slightly thickened, glistening and reduced by about half, 6 to 8 min. Remove from heat. Add pork chops, flip to coat in sauce, then serve drizzled with pan sauce along with roasted vegetables. Sprinkle pork chops with **chopped parsley** if desired.

SERVES 4 *About 570 cal, 31 g fat (9 g sat), 45 g pro, 590 mg sodium, 27 g carb, 4 g fiber*

Moroccan-Spiced Skillet Chicken and Couscous

ACTIVE **20 MIN.** | TOTAL **35 MIN.**

INGREDIENTS

CHICKEN BREASTS
4 6-oz boneless, skinless
chicken breasts

RAS EL HANOUT
1 Tbsp (see Tip)

PRESERVED LEMON
¼ lemon, pulp scraped
and discarded; rind finely
chopped (about 1 Tbsp)

TOMATO PASTE
2 Tbsp

PEARL COUSCOUS
1 cup quick-cooking

1. Place chicken breasts in large bowl and toss with **1 Tbsp olive oil**, then ras el hanout and ¼ tsp each kosher salt and pepper to coat.

2. Heat **1 Tbsp oil** in a large deep skillet or Dutch oven on medium. Add chicken breast and cook, undisturbed, until golden brown, 7 to 8 min. Flip and cook until other side is golden brown, 2 to 3 min.; transfer to plate (chicken will finish cooking later).

3. Add **1 Tbsp oil** to skillet along with rind from preserved lemon; cook, stirring constantly, 15 to 30 sec. Add tomato paste and cook, stirring constantly, 1 min.

4. Add pearl couscous and stir to coat. In large measuring cup, whisk **1 tsp salt** into **1½ cups water** then stir into pearl couscous and bring to a boil. Nestle chicken breasts darker-sides up in couscous and add any juices from plate. Cover, reduce heat and simmer until pearl couscous has absorbed most of the liquid and chicken breasts are cooked through, 14 to 15 min. Sprinkle with **chopped cilantro** if desired.

SERVES 4 *About 410 cal, 13.5 g fat (2.5 g sat), 39 g pro, 710 mg sodium, 32 g carb, 1 g fiber*

BONUS IDEA	**Quick Dip:** *Whip up a tangy, citrusy party dip. In a food processor, pulse rind from ¼ preserved lemon (chopped), 1 scallion (chopped), ¼ cup cilantro, ¼ cup Greek yogurt, 1 tsp hot sauce and ¼ tsp kosher salt until finely chopped. Pulse in 1 avocado until almost smooth. Serve with chips.*
TEST KITCHEN TIP	*The ingredients in ras el hanout can vary, depending on brand. If yours does not contain cumin or cinnamon, mix 1 tsp ground cumin and 1/4 tsp ground cinnamon into the ras el hanout before adding it to chicken.*

Multicooker Coconut Beef Curry

ACTIVE 20 MIN. | **TOTAL 1 HR. 5 MIN.**

INGREDIENTS

RED ONION
1, sliced

RED PEPPER
1, sliced

BEEF CHUCK ROAST
2 lbs, well trimmed and
cut into 3-in. pieces

COCONUT MILK
1 14.5-oz can, well shaken

**THAI RED
CURRY PASTE**
3 Tbsp

1. Set multicooker (such as Instant Pot) to sauté on high and heat **1 Tbsp olive oil**. Add red onion and red pepper, season with **¼ tsp each kosher salt and pepper** and sauté until tender, about 5 min.; transfer to bowl.

2. Add **1 Tbsp oil** to multicooker. Season beef chuck roast with **¼ tsp each salt and pepper** and cook until browned on all sides, about 5 min.

3. In large measuring cup, whisk together coconut milk and red curry paste, add to multicooker and scrape up any browned bits. Press cancel. Lock lid and cook on high pressure, 35 min. Let release naturally for 10 min., then manually release any remaining pressure and open lid.

4. Using 2 forks, break up meat into pieces, then toss with red onion and red pepper. Serve curry with **white rice** (the rice will sop up *all* the deliciousness!). Boost It: Top each bowl with **cilantro**, **sliced red chiles** and a **lime wedge** to add even more flavor.

SERVES 6 *About 400 cal, 26 g fat (15.5 g sat), 35 g pro, 480 mg sodium, 7 g carb, 1 g fiber*

BONUS IDEA	**Leftover Lunch:** *Change up your instant ramen by stirring Thai curry paste into the broth.*
TEST KITCHEN TIP	*No multicooker? Follow the sauté and browning instructions using a Dutch oven on the stovetop on medium heat. Scrap up brown bits, cover, transfer to a 350°F oven and bake until beef easily pulls apart, about 2 hr.*

Tomato Soup with Parmesan Crostini

ACTIVE **10 MIN.** | TOTAL **1 HR. 20 MIN.**

INGREDIENTS

TOMATOES
2¾ lbs

GARLIC
8 cloves, peeled
and smashed

RED ONION
1, thinly sliced

BAGUETTE
½ small, sliced
½ in. thick

PARMESAN
3 Tbsp, finely grated

1. Heat oven to 325°F. Toss tomatoes, garlic and red onion with **2 Tbsp olive oil** and **½ tsp each kosher salt and pepper** on a large rimmed baking sheet. Roast until tomatoes are tender and juicy and red onion is tender, 60 to 70 min. Transfer vegetables to large pot; add **4 cups water** and bring to a boil. Using an immersion blender (or standard blender in batches), puree until smooth.

2. Heat broiler. Arrange baguette slices on baking sheet, top with Parmesan and broil until melted; serve with soup.

SERVES 4 *About 185 cal, 8.5 g fat (1.5 g sat), 6 g pro, 395 mg sodium, 24 g carb, 5 g fiber*

BONUS IDEA	**Leftover Lunch:** *Bought extra baguettes? Serve up pizza! Arrange oven rack in center position and heat broiler. Split baguette and arrange on a baking sheet cut sides up. Broil until light golden brown, 2 to 3 min. Reduce oven temp to 375°F and top bread as desired. (Hello, marinara, mozzarella and pepperoni!) Bake until warm and melted.*

Potato and Chorizo Tacos

ACTIVE 35 MIN. | **TOTAL 35 MIN.**

INGREDIENTS

MEXICAN CHORIZO
1 lb fresh, casings
discarded, meat crumbled
into small pieces

RUSSET POTATOES
1¼ lbs (2 medium), cut
into ¼-in. pieces

YELLOW ONION
1

CORN TORTILLAS
8 small, warmed

SALSA VERDE
½ cup

1. Heat **1 Tbsp olive oil** in a large cast-iron skillet on medium-high. Add Mexican chorizo and cook, undisturbed, until browned on bottom, about 3 min. Continue to cook, breaking up into very small pieces with wooden spoon and adjusting heat if burning, until very crisp and brown, 6 to 8 min. more. Using slotted spoon, transfer meat to bowl and pour off all but 1 Tbsp fat from skillet.

2. Meanwhile, microwave russet potatoes in a large bowl covered with damp paper towel until tender, 4 to 5 min.

3. Finely chop white onion and set ⅓ cup aside for topping. Arrange cooked russet potatoes in single layer in skillet and cook, stirring every few min., until golden brown, 5 to 7 min. Add remaining white onion and **½ tsp each kosher salt and pepper** and cook, tossing occasionally, until tender, 3 to 5 min.

4. Return Mexican chorizo to skillet and toss to combine. Spoon chorizo-potato mixture into corn tortillas, top with salsa verde and reserved white onion.

SERVES 4 *About 542 cal, 24 g fat (10 g sat), 25 g pro, 1203 mg sodium, 49 g carb, 5 g fiber*

BONUS IDEA	**Next-Day Breakfast:** *Make 1½ times the chorizo-potato filling and refrigerate the extra overnight. Reheat in a skillet on medium and serve with eggs topped with grated Cheddar.*

Pasta e Piselli

ACTIVE **25 MIN.** | TOTAL **25 MIN.**

INGREDIENTS

ONION
1 small, finely chopped

PARMESAN
wedge

DITALINI PASTA
2 cups

CHICKEN BOUILLON BASE
1 Tbsp reduced-sodium (we used Better than Bouillon)

FROZEN PEAS
1 cup

1. Heat **2 tsp olive oil** in a medium saucepan on medium. Add onion and cook, stirring occasionally, until tender and golden, 5 to 7 min.

2. Cut rind off Parmesan wedge. Add **3 cups hot water**, ditalini pasta, chicken-bouillon base and Parmesan rind to saucepan. Bring to a vigorous simmer and cook, stirring occasionally, until pasta is tender and most of liquid is absorbed, 10 to 12 min.

3. Stir in frozen peas and **¼ tsp pepper**. Remove from heat and discard Parmesan rind. Serve drizzled with **oil** and sprinkled with grated Parmesan.

SERVES 4 *About 299 cal, 7.5 g fat (1 g sat), 10 g pro, 608 mg sodium, 48 g carb, 4 g fiber*

BONUS IDEA	**Leftover Lunch:** *Whip up a quick batch of soup: Start with chicken bouillon base and water, then stir in frozen peas, chopped carrots, egg noodles, rotisserie chicken...whatever your heart desires!*

WEEK 2 DINNERS
Week-At-A-Glance

DAY 8
Pan-Fried Chicken with
Lemony Roasted Broccoli

DAY 9
Roasted Cod and Potatoes
with Chorizo Vinaigrette

DAY 10
Ravioli with Turkey Sausage
and Brussels Sprouts

DAY 11
Black Bean–Stuffed
Poblano Peppers

DAY 12
Kimchi and Spam Fried Rice

DAY 13
Classic Patty Melt

DAY 14
Linguine with Clams

NOTES

_____

_____

_____

_____

WEEK 2
Shopping List

Buy just what you need each week. Below are exact amounts of every ingredient you will need for Week 2.

PRODUCE
1½   lbs broccoli
12   oz Brussels sprouts
7   cloves garlic
3   large yellow onions
1   lemon
1½   lbs new potatoes
1   cup fresh flat-leaf parsley, chopped, plus more for serving
4   poblano peppers
1   shallot

MEAT & SEAFOOD
4   6-oz pieces boneless, skinless chicken breasts
1   lb ground beef chuck
1   oz chorizo
½   lb Italian turkey sausage
4   6-oz cod fillets

REFRIGERATED & DAIRY
1½   cups ripe kimchi
¼   cup grated Parmesan, plus more for serving
6   slices Swiss cheese
6   slices American cheese
1   lb cheese ravioli
¼   cup pico de gallo

BREAD & BAKERY
8   slices rye bread

PANTRY
12   oz linguine
6   cups cooked short-grain white rice
½   cup low-sodium chicken broth
2   15-oz cans black beans
2   6.5-oz cans minced or chopped clams
1   12-oz can Spam
1½   Tbsp soy sauce
2   tsp toasted sesame oil
2   Tbsp sherry vinegar
1   11.5-oz jar vegan queso
¼   cup all-purpose flour
½   cup dry white wine

COOKING STAPLES
1   stick butter
¾   cups olive oil, plus more for serving
1   tsp canola oil
   Kosher salt and black pepper

BOOST IT

Some recipes this week may call for these flavor boosters and we highly recommend sprinkling them in if you already have them on hand. If you don't, it's OK—all the recipes are great on their own!

- Fresh parsley
- Furikake
- Lemon

Pan-Fried Chicken with Lemony Roasted Broccoli

ACTIVE **25 MIN.** | TOTAL **30 MIN.**

INGREDIENTS

BROCCOLI
1½ lbs, cut into florets

GARLIC
2 cloves, thinly sliced

CHICKEN BREASTS
4 6-oz boneless, skinless chicken breasts, pounded to ½ in. thick

ALL-PURPOSE FLOUR
¼ cup

LEMON
1

1. Heat oven to 425°F. Toss broccoli and garlic with **1 Tbsp olive oil** and **¼ tsp each kosher salt and pepper** on a large rimmed baking sheet; roast 10 min.

2. Meanwhile, season chicken breasts with **¼ tsp each salt and pepper**, then coat in flour. Heat **1 Tbsp oil** in a large skillet on medium-high and cook chicken breasts until golden brown, 3 to 5 min. per side. Nestle chicken breasts among broccoli mixture on baking sheet and roast until chicken breasts are cooked through and broccoli is golden brown and tender, about 6 min. more.

3. Juice lemon, then cut into thin ½-in. pieces. Return skillet to medium heat; add **1 Tbsp oil**, then lemon pieces, and cook, stirring, until beginning to brown, about 3 min. Add lemon juice and **⅓ cup water** and cook, stirring and scraping up any browned bits. Spoon over chicken breasts and serve with broccoli.

SERVES 4 *About 365 cal, 15.5 g fat (2.5 g sat), 44 g pro, 375 mg sodium, 15 g carb, 5 g fiber*

BONUS IDEA	**Leftover Lunch:** *Cut up any remaining broccoli and chicken breasts and toss with grated provolone. Sandwich between your favorite roll or bread and cook in a skillet, weighted down with sandwich press or heavy skillet until cheese melts and bread is crisp.*

Roasted Cod and Potatoes with Chorizo Vinaigrette

ACTIVE **15 MIN.** | TOTAL **30 MIN.**

INGREDIENTS

NEW POTATOES
1½ lbs, halved

COD
4 6-oz fillets

CHORIZO
1 oz Spanish cured,
finely chopped

SHALLOT
1, finely chopped

SHERRY VINEGAR
2 Tbsp

1. Heat oven to 450°F. Coat a large rimmed baking sheet with **2 Tbsp olive oil**. On baking sheet, toss new potatoes with **½ tsp each kosher salt and pepper** and arrange cut sides down; roast 15 min.

2. Pat cod fillets dry with paper towel and season with **¼ tsp each salt and pepper**. Place cod fillets on baking sheet, moving new potatoes aside as necessary. Roast until cod fillets are opaque throughout and new potatoes are golden brown and tender, 7 to 9 min. more.

3. Meanwhile, heat **1 tsp oil** in a small skillet on medium. Add Spanish cured chorizo and cook until crispy, 2 to 3 min.

4. Remove skillet from heat and add shallot, tossing to combine. Stir in sherry vinegar. Serve over cod fillets and new potatoes. Sprinkle with **chopped parsley** if desired.

SERVES 4 *About 355 cal, 11.5 g fat (2.5 g sat), 32 g pro, 595 mg sodium, 33 g carb, 3 g fiber*

BONUS IDEA	**Pasta Perfecto:** *A bit of cured chorizo can also amp up a weeknight pasta. Brown it in a skillet on medium, then stir in your favorite marinara until heated through (fold in baby spinach or kale if you have any). Toss with pappardelle or fettuccine and serve dolloped with ricotta.*

Ravioli with Turkey Sausage and Brussels Sprouts

ACTIVE **20 MIN.** | TOTAL **20 MIN.**

INGREDIENTS

CHEESE RAVIOLI
1 lb

ITALIAN TURKEY SAUSAGE
½ lb, casings removed

BRUSSELS SPROUTS
12 oz, trimmed and sliced

CHICKEN BROTH
½ cup low-sodium

PARMESAN
¼ cup grated

1. Cook cheese ravioli per pkg. directions.

2. Meanwhile, heat **2 Tbsp olive oil** in a large skillet on medium-high. Add turkey sausage and cook, breaking up into small pieces with wooden spoon, until browned, 6 to 7 min.

3. Add Brussels sprouts, season with **½ tsp kosher salt and ¼ tsp pepper** and cook, tossing often, 2 min. Add chicken broth and bring to a simmer.

4. Add Parmesan to skillet and gently toss to combine. Serve turkey sausage and Brussels sprout mixture over cheese ravioli and sprinkle with additional Parmesan and **cracked pepper**.

SERVES 4 *About 295 cal, 15 g fat (2 g sat), 16 g pro, 1045 mg sodium, 24 g carb, 4 g fiber*

Black Bean – Stuffed Poblano Peppers

ACTIVE **35 MIN.** | TOTAL **35 MIN.**

INGREDIENTS

POBLANO PEPPERS
4

GARLIC
2 cloves

BLACK BEANS
2 15-oz cans,
including liquid

VEGAN QUESO
11.5-oz jar (about
1¼ cups)

PICO DE GALLO
¼ cup

1. Position rack 4 in. from broiler and heat broiler. Cut poblano peppers in half through stems and discard seeds. Toss poblano peppers with **1 Tbsp olive oil** and **¼ tsp each kosher salt and pepper** on a large rimmed baking sheet. Arrange cut sides down and broil 3 min. Flip and broil until charred and tender, 2 to 4 min.

2. Meanwhile, grate garlic into medium saucepan. Add **2 Tbsp unsalted butter** and cook on low to melt butter. Add black beans and **½ cup water** and bring to a simmer. Simmer, stirring occasionally, until thickened, 11 to 14 min.; remove from heat.

3. Heat vegan queso per pkg. directions. Spoon 3 Tbsp each onto 4 plates and top with poblano peppers, cut sides up.

4. Spoon black beans into poblano peppers, top with remaining vegan queso, then top with pico de gallo.

SERVES 4 *About 505 cal, 18.5 g fat (4.5 g sat), 25 g pro, 1170 mg sodium, 64 g carb, 22 g fiber*

Kimchi and Spam Fried Rice

ACTIVE **35 MIN.** | TOTAL **35 MIN.**

INGREDIENTS

SPAM
1 12-oz can, cut lengthwise
into ½-in.-thick slabs,
then crosswise into
¼-in. strips

KIMCHI
1½ cups ripe, squeezed
well of liquid and
chopped (reserve 5 Tbsp
kimchi liquid

WHITE RICE
6 cups cooked short-
grain, preferably day-old

SOY SAUCE
1½ Tbsp

**TOASTED
SESAME OIL**
2 tsp

1. Heat large nonstick skillet on medium. Add Spam to skillet in single layer. Cook, undisturbed, until bottom is golden brown, 3 to 4 min. Toss and continue to cook, tossing a few times, until golden brown and beginning to crisp, 5 to 6 min. more. Transfer to large plate.

2. Add **1 tsp canola oil** to the same skillet. Add kimchi and cook, tossing occasionally, until beginning to caramelize and char, 4 to 5 min. Add cooked white rice and cook, breaking up rice with wooden spatula and tossing to combine.

3. Add soy sauce, toasted sesame oil and reserved kimchi liquid to skillet and fold to combine. Cook, tossing occasionally, until white rice is hot, 4 to 5 min. Fold in Spam and cook until warmed through, about 1 min. more. Sprinkle with **furikake** if desired.

SERVES 4 *About 685 cal, 28.5 g fat (9.5 g sat), 19 g pro, 1765 mg sodium, 85 g carb, 4 g fiber*

Classic Patty Melt

ACTIVE 25 MIN. | TOTAL 1 HR.

INGREDIENTS

YELLOW ONIONS
3 large, thinly sliced

GROUND BEEF CHUCK
1 lb

RYE BREAD
8 thin slices

SWISS CHEESE
6 thin slices

AMERICAN CHEESE
6 thin slices

1. Melt **2 Tbsp unsalted butter** in a large skillet on medium-low. Add onions, season with **½ tsp kosher salt and ¼ tsp pepper**, and cook, covered, stirring occasionally, until tender, 8 to 10 min. Increase heat to medium and cook, stirring frequently, until deep golden brown, 30 to 40 min. (Add **1 to 2 Tbsp** water if onions stick or pan browns).

2. Shape ground beef chuck into 4 thin patties slightly larger than slices of rye bread. Heat large cast-iron skillet on medium-high. Season patties with **½ tsp each salt and pepper** and cook 2 min. per side; transfer to plate.

3. Wipe out skillet and return to medium-low heat. Spread **3 Tbsp softened unsalted butter** on one side of the rye bread slices.

4. In 2 batches, place 2 slices rye bread, butter sides down, in skillet. Top each with 1½ slices Swiss cheese, 1 patty, ¼ cup caramelized onions, 1½ slices American cheese and second slice of rye bread, butter side up. Place small skillet (wrapped in foil) on top of sandwiches to press and cook until rye bread is golden brown and crisp, 3 min. per side.

SERVES 4 *About 655 cal, 40.5 g fat (14.5 g sat), 36 g pro, 1, 190 mg sodium, 33 g carb, 4 g fiber*

BONUS IDEA	**Easy Breakfast:** *Fold leftover caramelized onions, sliced ham, any chopped tender herbs and your favorite cheese into beaten eggs. Transfer to an oiled cast-iron skillet and bake at 375°F until set around edges and still slightly wobbly in the middle.*

Linguine with Clams

ACTIVE **20 MIN.** | TOTAL **20 MIN.**

INGREDIENTS

LINGUINE
12 oz

CLAMS
2 6.5-oz cans minced or
chopped

GARLIC
3 large cloves,
thinly sliced

DRY WHITE WINE
½ cup

FLAT-LEAF PARSLEY
1 cup, chopped, plus more
for serving

1. Cook linguine per pkg. directions. Reserve ½ cup pasta cooking water, then drain pasta.

2. Meanwhile, drain minced or chopped clams and reserve clam juice (you should have about 1 cup juice).

3. Heat **¼ cup olive oil** and garlic in a large skillet on medium, stirring occasionally, until garlic is just golden at edges (do not let brown), 1 ½ to 2 min. Carefully add dry white wine and cook until reduced by half, 1 ½ to 2 min.

4. Add reserved clam juice, leaving behind any grit, and cook until sauce is slightly reduced, 2 to 3 min. If linguine is not ready yet, remove skillet from heat.

5. If needed, reheat sauce on medium. Add linguine, minced or chopped clams, **½ tsp pepper** and ¼ cup reserved pasta water to sauce and cook, tossing and adding reserved pasta water 1 Tbsp at a time as needed, until linguine has absorbed most of liquid and is coated with a glossy sauce, about 2 min. Toss with parsley.

6. Serve drizzled with **oil** and topped with additional parsley and pepper. For extra brightness, sprinkle **grated lemon zest** and squeeze **lemon juice** over linguine if desired.

SERVES *4 About 505 cal, 18.5 g fat (2.5 g sat), 16 g pro, 420 mg sodium, 69 g carb, 4 g fiber*

WEEK 3 DINNERS
Week-At-A-Glance

DAY 15
Sheet Pan Salmon,
Broccoli and Rice

DAY 16
Seared Chicken with Cheesy
Spinach and Artichokes

DAY 17
Sausage Sheet Pan Dinner

DAY 18
Grilled Mushroom and
Scallion Pasta

DAY 19
Skillet Chicken Enchiladas

DAY 20
Pea and Ricotta Omelets

DAY 21
Barbecue Pulled
Jackfruit Sandwiches

NOTES

_____

_____

_____

_____

WEEK 3
Shopping List

PRODUCE
1   clove garlic
1   medium white onion
2   medium red onions
1   lb baby yellow potatoes
12 oz broccoli crowns
20 oz cremini mushrooms
1   bunch spinach
2   oz (about 4 cups) baby arugula
1½ bunch scallions
3   Tbsp mint leaves
2   Tbsp chives
1   12-oz pkg. tricolor
    coleslaw mix

MEAT & SEAFOOD
4   5-oz skinless salmon fillets
4   6-oz boneless, skinless
    chicken breasts
6   small links Italian sausage
    (about 1½ lbs total)
3   cups shredded
    rotisserie chicken

REFRIGERATED & DAIRY
8   large eggs
½   5.2-oz pkg. Garlic & Herb soft
    cheese (we used Boursin)
8   oz pepper Jack cheese
4   Tbsp ricotta

FROZEN
1   cup frozen peas

BREAD & BAKERY
4   vegan brioche-style buns
6   corn tortillas

PANTRY
12 oz mezzi rigatoni
1   cup long-grain white rice
1   14-oz can artichoke halves
2   14-oz cans young green
    jackfruit, in brine or water,
    not syrup
5   Tbsp teriyaki sauce
1¾ cups barbecue sauce
    (we used Dinosaur)
2   cups mild red
    enchilada sauce
2   Tbsp Italian dressing
¼   cup vegan ranch dressing
    (we used Drew's)
⅓   cup nutritional yeast
½   cup dry white wine

COOKING STAPLES
8   Tbsp olive oil
    Kosher salt and black pepper

BOOST IT

Some recipes this week may call for these flavor boosters and we highly recommend sprinkling them in if you already have them on hand. If you don't, it's OK—all the recipes are great on their own!

- Fresh cilantro
- Lemon
- Scallions
- Sesame seeds
- Avocado

Sheet Pan Salmon, Broccoli and Rice

ACTIVE **20 MIN.** | TOTAL **40 MIN.**

INGREDIENTS

WHITE RICE
1 cup long-grain

TERIYAKI SAUCE
5 Tbsp, divided, plus more
for serving

BROCCOLI
12 oz crowns, trimmed
and cut into ½-in. pieces

SALMON
4 5-oz skinless fillets

SCALLIONS
3, thinly sliced

1. Heat oven to 425°F. On large rimmed baking sheet (for even cooking, make sure it's level and not warped), stir together white rice, **2½ cups water** and **¼ tsp kosher salt**. Roast for 10 min.

2. Meanwhile, whisk together **½ Tbsp olive oil** and 1 Tbsp teriyaki sauce in a medium bowl. Add broccoli crowns and toss to coat. Stir rice, scatter broccoli crowns on top and roast 6 min. more.

3. Nestle salmon fillets in rice. Spoon 1 Tbsp teriyaki sauce over each salmon fillet and bake until opaque throughout, 8 to 11 min. Serve salmon fillets, broccoli crowns and white rice drizzled with additional teriyaki sauce and sprinkled with scallions. For added crunch, sprinkle with **sesame seeds** if desired.

SERVES 4 *About 400 cal, 14.5 g fat (2.5 g sat), 36 g pro, 665 mg sodium, 31 g carb, 2 g fiber*

BONUS IDEA	**Leftover Lunch:** *Toss teriyaki sauce with slaw mix, then fold in shredded chicken, canned salmon or roasted tofu.*

Seared Chicken with Cheesy Spinach and Artichokes

ACTIVE **30 MIN.** | TOTAL **30 MIN.**

INGREDIENTS

ARTICHOKE HALVES
1 14-oz can, patted dry

CHICKEN BREASTS
4 6-oz boneless, skinless chicken breasts, pounded to ½ in. thick

DRY WHITE WINE
½ cup

GARLIC AND HERB SOFT CHEESE
½ 5.2-oz pkg. (we used Garlic & Fine Herbs Boursin)

SPINACH
1 bunch, thick stems discarded, roughly chopped

1. Heat **1 Tbsp olive oil** in a large skillet on medium-high. Add artichoke halves, cut sides down, season with **¼ tsp each kosher salt and pepper** and cook until golden brown, 3 min. Transfer to plate.

2. Heat **1 Tbsp oil** in the same skillet on medium. Season chicken breasts with **½ tsp salt and ¼ tsp pepper** and cook until golden brown and cooked through, 5 to 7 min. per side. Transfer to plates.

3. Add dry white wine to skillet; cook, scraping up any browned bits, 2 min. Stir in garlic and herb soft cheese until melted. Fold in spinach to wilt, then fold in artichoke halves. Serve with chicken breasts.

SERVES 4 *About 380 cal, 19 g fat (7 g sat), 42 g pro, 755 mg sodium, 7 g carb, 1 g fiber*

BONUS IDEA	**Leftover Lunch:** *For the fastest pasta sauce, toss some garlic and herb soft cheese with freshly cooked spaghetti (note: noodles should be hot!) along with a squeeze of lemon, a pinch each kosher salt and pepper and a handful of baby spinach or chopped spinach.*

Sausage Sheet Pan Dinner

ACTIVE **15 MIN.** | TOTAL **40 MIN.**

INGREDIENTS

BABY YELLOW POTATOES
1 lb, halved

RED ONIONS
2 medium, cut into ½-in.-thick wedges

ITALIAN SAUSAGE
6 small links (about 1½ lbs)

BABY ARUGULA
2 oz (about 4 cups)

ITALIAN DRESSING
2 Tbsp

1. Heat oven to 450°F. Brush a large rimmed baking sheet with **1 Tbsp olive oil**. Arrange baby yellow potatoes cut sides down on baking sheet with red onions and roast 15 min. Flip red onions, then continue to roast until red onions and baby yellow potatoes are golden brown and tender, 10 to 14 min. more.

2. Meanwhile, heat **½ Tbsp oil** in a large ovenproof skillet on medium. Add Italian sausage and cook, turning occasionally, until browned, 5 to 6 min. Transfer skillet to oven and roast until cooked through, 10 to 15 min. more.

3. Scatter baby arugula over potato mixture, drizzle with Italian dressing and gently toss to combine. Serve alongside sausage or slice sausage and gently toss together.

SERVES 4 *About 460 cal, 29 g fat (8.5 g sat), 20 g pro, 730 mg sodium, 30 g carb, 3 g fiber*

Grilled Mushroom and Scallion Pasta

ACTIVE 25 MIN. | TOTAL **30 MIN.**

INGREDIENTS

MEZZI RIGATONI
12 oz

CREMINI MUSHROOMS
20 oz, trimmed

SCALLIONS
1 bunch, trimmed

GARLIC
1 clove

NUTRITIONAL YEAST
1/3 cup

1. Heat grill to medium-high. Cook mezzi rigatoni per pkg. directions. Reserve ¾ cup pasta cooking water, then drain pasta and return to pot.

2. Meanwhile, toss cremini mushrooms and scallions with **2 Tbsp olive oil** and **¾ tsp kosher salt** in a large bowl. Grill vegetables, turning occasionally, until charred and just tender, 2 to 3 min. for scallions and 5 to 8 min. for cremini mushrooms (depending on size). When cool enough to handle, cut scallions into 1-in. pieces and halve cremini mushrooms (quarter if large). Grill **lemon halves** until charred to serve alongside pasta if desired.

3. Finely grate garlic over hot pasta and toss to combine. Toss with nutritional yeast, ½ tsp each salt and pepper and ½ cup reserved pasta water, adding more if pasta seems dry. Add mushrooms and scallions then toss with pasta. Sprinkle with **cracked pepper** and serve with lemon halves if desired.

SERVES 4 *About 440 cal, 9 g fat (1 g sat), 21 g pro, 615 mg sodium, 74 g carb, 7 g fiber*

Skillet Chicken Enchiladas

ACTIVE 15 MIN. | **TOTAL 40 MIN.**

INGREDIENTS

WHITE ONION
1 medium

ROTISSERIE CHICKEN
3 cups, shredded

CORN TORTILLAS
6, sliced into ½-in.-wide strips, then halved crosswise

RED ENCHILADA SAUCE
2 cups mild

PEPPER JACK CHEESE
8 oz coarsely grated (about 2½ cups), divided

1. Arrange racks in upper third and middle of oven and heat oven to 375°F. Chop white onion then transfer all but ½ cup to large bowl. Reserve remaining ½ cup for topping.

2. Add rotisserie chicken and corn tortillas and toss together.

3. Drizzle with red enchilada sauce and toss to coat.

4. Fold 1¼ cups pepper Jack cheese into chicken mixture. Transfer mixture to 10-in. stainless-steel or cast-iron skillet, spread in even layer and top with remaining pepper Jack cheese. Bake on middle rack until pepper Jack cheese is melted and sauce is bubbling, 20 to 22 min. Remove skillet from oven.

5. Heat broiler. Place skillet on top oven rack and broil until pepper Jack cheese is golden brown, 2 to 3 min. Sprinkle with remaining white onion and serve. Sprinkle with **chopped cilantro** if desired.

SERVES 4 *About 490 cal, 33.5 g fat (15 g sat), 34 g pro, 1389 mg sodium, 27 g carb, 3 g fiber*

Pea and Ricotta Omelets

ACTIVE **20 MIN.** | TOTAL **20 MIN.**

INGREDIENTS

FROZEN PEAS
1 cup, thawed, divided

EGGS
8 large, divided

RICOTTA
4 Tbsp, divided

CHIVE
2 Tbsp, thinly sliced

MINT
3 Tbsp, sliced, divided

1. Heat oven to 350°F. Mash ½ cup frozen peas in small bowl.

2. Transfer half of mashed peas to large bowl along with 4 large eggs, 1 Tbsp each ricotta and chives, **¼ tsp kosher salt and ⅛ tsp pepper** and whisk until well combined.

3. Heat **1 Tbsp olive oil** in medium ovenproof nonstick skillet on medium. Add egg mixture and quickly stir until eggs begin to set and form medium-size curds, 1 to 2 min. Top with ¼ cup whole frozen peas, transfer to oven and bake until eggs are set, 1 to 2 min.

4. Slide omelet onto plate, folding in half, then top with 1 Tbsp ricotta and 1½ Tbsp mint. Halve omelet and transfer one piece to a second plate. Repeat with remaining ingredients to make second omelet.

SERVES 4 (½ omelet each) *About 258 cal, 18.5 g fat (5.5 g sat), 16 g pro, 397 mg sodium, 6 g carb, 2 g fiber*

Barbecue Pulled Jackfruit Sandwiches

ACTIVE **15 MIN.** | TOTAL **35 MIN.**

INGREDIENTS

BARBECUE SAUCE
1¾ cups (we used
Dinosaur Bar-B-Que)

JACKFRUIT
2 14-oz cans young green,
in brine or water (not
syrup); rinsed

COLESLAW MIX
1 12-oz bag tricolor

**VEGAN RANCH
DRESSING**
¼ cup (we used Drew's)

**BRIOCHE-STYLE
BUNS**
4 vegan

1. In medium saucepan, stir together barbecue sauce and **½ cup water**. Add young green jackfruit and bring to a simmer. Cover and gently simmer, stirring occasionally, until young green jackfruit is tender and easily pulls apart and sauce has slightly reduced, 25 to 30 min. Remove from heat. Remove young green jackfruit with slotted spoon and shred using 2 forks; thinly slice any thick core. Return to pot.

2. Meanwhile, toss coleslaw mix with vegan ranch dressing and **¼ tsp pepper** in large bowl. Refrigerate until ready to use.

3. Divide jackfruit among vegan brioche-style buns and top with slaw. Add **sliced avocado** for a creamy boost if desired.

SERVES 4 *About 365 cal, 12 g fat (1 g sat), 6 g pro, 1135 mg sodium, 57 g carb, 4 g fiber*

WEEK 4 DINNERS
Week-At-A-Glance

DAY 22
Cod in Parchment with
Orange-Leek Couscous

DAY 23
Oil and Vinegar Chicken
Cutlet Sandwiches

DAY 24
Steak with Harissa
Butter Carrots

DAY 25
Shrimp and Asparagus
Stir-Fry

DAY 26
Linguine Carbonara

DAY 27
Chicken Shawarma

DAY 28
Shakshuka

NOTES

WEEK 4
Shopping List

PRODUCE
1   clove garlic
1   yellow onion
2   medium red onions
½   small red onion
1   leek
1¾   lbs rainbow carrots
1   lb asparagus
1   lb cherry or grape tomatoes
3   cups baby kale
6   cups baby spinach
3   scallions
½   cup flat-leaf parsley
1   lemon
1   navel orange

MEAT & SEAFOOD
1   to 1¼ lbs hanger steak
1   lb boneless, skinless chicken breasts
4   large boneless, skinless chicken thighs
6   oz sliced bacon
4   5-oz skinless cod fillets
1   lb large peeled and deveined

REFRIGERATED & DAIRY
11   large eggs
½   cup freshly grated Parmesan, plus more for serving
1   cup tzatziki, plus more for serving

BREAD & BAKERY
1   baguette
4   pitas or flatbreads

PANTRY
12   oz linguine
1   cup couscous
1   Tbsp red wine vinegar
1   Tbsp honey
2   Tbsp gochujang
¾   tsp harissa
1   tsp coriander seeds
1   tsp ground cumin
1½   Tbsp shawarma seasoning

COOKING STAPLES
2   Tbsp unsalted butter
9   Tbsp olive oil
    Kosher salt and black pepper

BOOST IT

Some recipes this week may call for these flavor boosters and we highly recommend sprinkling them in if you already have them on hand. If you don't, it's OK—all the recipes are great on their own!

- Grape tomatoes
- Baby spinach
- Pita or flatbread

Cod in Parchment with Orange-Leek Couscous

ACTIVE 15 MIN. | **TOTAL 30 MIN.**

INGREDIENTS

COUSCOUS
1 cup

ORANGE
1

LEEK
1, white and light green
parts only, cut into 1/2-in.-
thick half-moons

BABY KALE
3 cups

COD
4 5-oz skinless fillets

1. Heat oven to 425°F. Cut eight 12-in. squares of parchment. Put 4 squares on 2 baking sheets. In large bowl, combine couscous with **3/4 cup water**.

2. Cut orange in half, then peel a half and coarsely chop fruit. Fold orange into couscous along with leek and baby kale.

3. Divide couscous mixture among the 4 parchment squares and top each with 1 cod fillet. Drizzle with **1 Tbsp olive oil**; sprinkle with **1/2 tsp kosher salt and 1/4 tsp pepper**; squeeze juice from remaining orange half over top.

4. Cover each cod fillet with another piece of parchment; fold each edge up and under 3 times, then tuck each corner underneath itself to seal. Roast 12 min.

5. Transfer packets to plates. Using scissors and watching out for steam, very carefully cut an "X" in center of each packet and fold back triangles to serve.

SERVES 4 *About 340 cal, 5 g fat (1 g sat), 32 g pro, 330 mg sodium, 40 g carb, 3 g fiber*

Oil and Vinegar Chicken Cutlet Sandwiches

ACTIVE **20 MIN.** | TOTAL **20 MIN.**

INGREDIENTS

RED ONION
½ small, thinly sliced

RED WINE VINEGAR
1 Tbsp

CHICKEN BREASTS
1 lb boneless, skinless
chicken breasts, cut into
6 thin cutlets

BABY SPINACH
6 cups

BAGUETTE
1, quartered, split
and toasted

1. In medium bowl, toss red onion with red wine vinegar and ⅛ **tsp each kosher salt and pepper**; let sit, tossing occasionally.

2. Heat 1 Tbsp olive oil in a large skillet on medium-high. Season chicken breasts with ½ **tsp each salt and pepper** and cook until browned and cooked through, about 2 min. per side; transfer to cutting board.

3. Add baby spinach to skillet, season with pinch each **salt and pepper** and cook until just beginning to wilt, about 2 min.

4. Slice chicken breasts and sandwich between baguette halves with spinach and onions.

SERVES 4 *About 330 cal, 7 g fat (1 g sat), 33 g pro, 705 mg sodium, 32 g carb, 3 g fiber*

Steak with Harissa Butter Carrots

ACTIVE **25 MIN.** | TOTAL **50 MIN.**

INGREDIENTS

RAINBOW CARROTS
1¾ lbs, peeled and
halved crosswise, thick
ends halved lengthwise
or quartered if very thick

CORIANDER SEED
1 tsp, crushed

HONEY
1 Tbsp

HANGER STEAK
1 to 1¼ lbs, trimmed

HARISSA
¾ tsp, mild

1. Place large rimmed baking sheet in oven and heat oven to 425°F. Toss rainbow carrots with **1 Tbsp olive oil**, coriander seeds and **¼ tsp each kosher salt and pepper** in a large bowl.

2. Carefully arrange carrot mixture on preheated baking sheet and roast until golden brown and tender, 20 to 28 min., depending on thickness of carrots. Immediately drizzle with honey and toss to combine.

3. Meanwhile, heat **1 Tbsp oil** in a large cast-iron skillet on medium-high. Season hanger steak with **½ tsp each salt and pepper**. Cook to desired doneness, 2 to 4 min. on all sides for medium-rare. Transfer to cutting board and let rest at least 5 min. before slicing.

4. Mash **2 Tbsp softened unsalted butter** with harissa and **pinch each of salt and pepper** in a small bowl. Top steak with harissa butter and serve with roasted carrots.

SERVES 4 *About 410 cal, 24 g fat (9 g sat), 30 g pro, 595 mg sodium, 21 g carb, 5 g fiber*

Shrimp and Asparagus Stir-Fry

ACTIVE **25 MIN.** | TOTAL **25 MIN.**

INGREDIENTS

GOCHUJANG
2 Tbsp

SCALLIONS
3

ASPARAGUS
1 lb, trimmed and cut into
2-in. pieces

SHRIMP
1 lb large peeled and
deveined

LEMON
1, plus wedges for serving

1. In small bowl, stir together gochujang and **3 to 4 Tbsp water** until pourable; set aside. Cut white and light green parts of scallions into 2-in. pieces; thinly slice dark green parts.

2. Heat ½ **Tbsp olive oil** in a large skillet on medium-high. Add asparagus, scallion white and light green parts and ¼ **tsp kosher salt** and cook, without stirring, 2 min. Toss and continue to cook, tossing occasionally, until just tender, 2 to 3 min. more; transfer to plate and wipe out skillet.

3. Add ½ **Tbsp oil** to the skillet and heat on medium. Add shrimp and cook, without stirring, 2 min. Flip and cook 1 min. more. Return asparagus and scallions to skillet along with gochujang mixture and cook, tossing, until shrimp is opaque throughout and coated in sauce, 30 to 60 sec.

4. Remove from heat and toss with 1 Tbsp fresh lemon juice. Sprinkle with scallion dark green parts and serve with lemon wedges.

SERVES 4 *About 445 cal, 11.5 g fat (3.5 g sat), 17 g pro, 464 mg sodium, 67 g carb, 5 g fiber*

Linguine Carbonara

ACTIVE **15 MIN.** | TOTAL **25 MIN.**

INGREDIENTS

LINGUINE
12 oz

BACON
6 oz sliced, cut into
1-in. pieces

EGGS
3 large yolks

PARMESAN
½ cup freshly grated,
plus more for serving

FLAT-LEAF PARSLEY
½ cup, chopped

1. Cook linguine per pkg. directions. Reserve ¾ cup pasta cooking water, then drain pasta.

2. Cook bacon in large skillet on medium until crisp, about 5 to 6 min. Transfer to paper towel–lined plate.

3. Whisk together egg yolks, Parmesan and ¼ **tsp each kosher salt and pepper** in large bowl. Gradually whisk in ¼ cup reserved warm pasta water. Add hot pasta and toss to coat, adding more reserved pasta water if pasta seems dry.

4. Fold in parsley and bacon. Sprinkle with lots of **cracked pepper** and additional Parmesan.

SERVES 4 *About 470 cal, 13.5 g fat (5 g sat), 22 g pro, 555 mg sodium, 66 g carb, 3 g fiber*

Chicken Shawarma

ACTIVE **30 MIN.** | TOTAL **30 MIN.**

INGREDIENTS

RED ONIONS
2 medium

CHICKEN THIGHS
4 large boneless, skinless
chicken thighs (about
1¼ lbs total)

**SHAWARMA
SEASONING**
1½ Tbsp, plus more
for serving

PITA OR FLATBREAD
4, warmed

TZATZIKI
1 cup, plus more
for serving

1. Arrange racks in middle and top third of oven and heat broiler. Finely chop one-quarter of a red onion and set aside for topping. Cut the remaining red onions into 1½-in. pieces and place on large rimmed baking sheet. Toss with **1 Tbsp olive oil** and **¼ tsp each kosher salt and pepper**.

2. Toss chicken thighs with **1 Tbsp oil**, then 1½ Tbsp shawarma seasoning and **¼ tsp each salt and pepper** in a medium bowl. Nestle chicken thighs among red onions and broil on middle rack until chicken thighs and red onions begin to brown, 12 to 15 min. Transfer baking sheet to upper rack and broil until browned and chicken thighs are cooked through, 2 to 3 min. more. Let chicken thighs rest 5 min. before chopping.

3. Top pitas or flatbreads with tzatziki, chopped chicken thighs and cooked red onions. Sprinkle with reserved raw red onion then top with more tzatziki and more shawarma seasoning before serving. Top with **sliced grape tomatoes** if desired.

SERVES *4 About 410 cal, 24 g fat (9 g sat), 30 g pro, 595 mg sodium, 21 g carb, 5 g fiber*

Shakshuka

ACTIVE 15 MIN. | TOTAL **35 MIN.**

INGREDIENTS

YELLOW ONION
1, finely chopped

GARLIC
1 clove, finely chopped

GROUND CUMIN
1 tsp

CHERRY OR GRAPE TOMATOES
1 lb, halved if large

EGGS
8 large

1. Heat oven to 400°F. Heat **2 Tbsp olive oil** in a large ovenproof skillet on medium. Add yellow onions and sauté until golden brown and tender, 6 to 8 min.

2. Stir in garlic, ground cumin and **½ tsp each kosher salt and pepper** and cook 1 min.

3. Stir in cherry or grape tomatoes, transfer to oven and roast 10 min.

4. Stir vegetable mixture, then make 8 small wells and, one at a time, carefully crack an egg into each well. Bake eggs to desired doneness, 7 to 8 min. for slightly runny yolks. Sprinkle baked eggs with **finely chopped baby spinach** and serve with **warmed pita or flatbread** if desired.

SERVES 4 *About 235 cal, 16.5 g fat (4 g sat), 14 g pro, 390 mg sodium, 8 g carb, 2 g fiber*

WEEK 5 DINNERS
Week-At-A-Glance

DAY 29
Air Fryer Fish and Chips

DAY 30
Chicken à L'Orange

DAY 31
Seared Pork Chops with
Cherries and Spinach

DAY 32
Citrus-Marinated Steak
and Crispy Potatoes

DAY 33
Sheet Pan Asparagus Frittata

DAY 34
Ham and Brie Quesadillas

DAY 35
Pea Pesto Pappardelle

NOTES

_____

_____

_____

_____

_____

WEEK 5
Shopping List

PRODUCE

2	small red onions
8	shallots
1¼	lbs yellow potatoes
1	lb green beans
1	lb asparagus
2	bunches spinach
2	cups baby spinach
2	lemons
1	orange
1	cup cherries

MEAT & SEAFOOD

2	12-oz strip steaks
4	6-oz boneless pork chops
1	3- to 3½-lbs whole chicken
1½	lbs skinless cod fillets
4	oz sliced ham

REFRIGERATED & DAIRY

14	large eggs
1	cup milk
2½	oz goat cheese
4	oz Brie
½	cup ricotta
¼	cup grated Parmesan
½	cup chimichurri

FROZEN

1	16-oz bag, plus 1½ cups frozen peas

BREAD & BAKERY

2	large flour tortillas

PANTRY

12	oz pappardelle
1	Tbsp white wine vinegar
4	tsp Dijon mustard
2	tsp whole-grain mustard
8	cornichons
½	cup orange marmalade
2	5-oz pkgs. salt and vinegar potato chips
¼	cup dry white wine

COOKING STAPLES

6	Tbsp olive oil, plus more for serving
	Kosher salt and black pepper

BOOST IT

Some recipes this week may call for these flavor boosters and we highly recommend sprinkling them in if you already have them on hand. If you don't, it's OK—all the recipes are great on their own!

- Chives
- Watercress
- Red onion
- Lemons

Air Fryer Fish and Chips

ACTIVE 15 MIN. | TOTAL **20 MIN.**

INGREDIENTS

EGGS
2 large, whites

SALT AND VINEGAR POTATO CHIPS
2 5-oz pkgs. (about 4 cups)

COD
1½ lbs skinless fillets, cut into 3-in. pieces

FROZEN PEAS
16 oz, thawed

LEMON
1, plus wedges for serving

1. Heat air fryer to 400°F. In shallow bowl, beat egg whites and **1 Tbsp water**.

2. Crush potato chips and place in second shallow bowl.

3. Dip cod fillets in egg whites, letting excess drip off, then in crushed potato chips, pressing gently to help adhere. Spray air fryer basket with **olive oil**, arrange cod fillets in basket and air-fry until fish is golden brown and opaque throughout, about 10 min.

4. Meanwhile, microwave frozen peas in medium bowl on medium, 2 min. Toss with 1 tsp lemon zest, 2 Tbsp lemon juice, **1 Tbsp oil** and ½ tsp **each kosher salt and pepper**, then mash. Serve with cod and lemon wedges.

SERVES 4 *About 661 cal, 30 g fat (4.5 g sat), 40 g pro, 916 mg sodium, 54 g carb, 8 g fiber*

TEST KITCHEN TIP	*No air fryer? Heat oven to 450°F. Coat fish as directed and transfer to a large rimmed baking sheet rubbed with 1 Tbsp olive oil. Roast until fish is golden brown and opaque throughout, 10 to 12 min.*

Chicken à L'Orange

ACTIVE **20 MIN.** | TOTAL **50 MIN.**

INGREDIENTS

SHALLOTS
8, halved lengthwise or
quartered if large

WHOLE CHICKEN
3 to 3½ lbs

**ORANGE
MARMALADE**
½ cup

**WHITE WINE
VINEGAR**
1 Tbsp

GREEN BEANS
1 lb, trimmed

1. Heat oven to 425°F. Toss shallots with **1 Tbsp olive oil** and **¼ tsp each kosher salt and pepper** in a large shallow roasting pan.

2. Cut whole chicken into 10 pieces (breasts halved).

3. Whisk together orange marmalade, white wine vinegar, **1 Tbsp oil** and **¼ tsp each salt and pepper** in a large bowl. Add chicken and toss to coat. Arrange chicken in roasting pan, nestling pieces among shallots. Roast until chicken is browned and cooked through and shallots are tender, 25 to 35 min.

4. Meanwhile, fill large pot with **1 inch water**, place vegetable steamer basket inside and bring water to boil. Reduce heat to simmer, add ½ lb green beans and cook, covered, until just tender, 4 to 6 min. Transfer to platter and repeat with remaining ½ lb green beans, adding additional water as needed. Serve with chicken.

SERVES 4 *About 620 cal, 29 g fat (7 g sat), 48 g pro, 410 mg sodium, 44 g carb, 5 g fiber*

Seared Pork Chops with Cherries and Spinach

ACTIVE **15 MIN.** | TOTAL **30 MIN.**

INGREDIENTS

PORK CHOP
4 6-oz boneless
pork chops

CHERRIES
1 cup, pitted and halved

DRY WHITE WINE
¼ cup

**WHOLE-GRAIN
MUSTARD**
2 tsp

SPINACH
2 bunches, thick
stems discarded

1. Heat **1 Tbsp olive oil** in a large skillet on medium. Pat pork chops dry with paper towel and season with **½ tsp each kosher salt and pepper**. Cook until golden brown and just cooked through, 8 to 10 min. per side; transfer to plates.

2. Add cherries to skillet and cook, stirring occasionally, until beginning to soften, about 2 min. Add dry white wine and cook until reduced to 1 Tbsp, about 2 min. more.

3. Stir in whole-grain mustard and **⅓ cup water**, then spinach, and cook, tossing, until beginning to wilt, about 2 min. Serve with pork.

SERVES 4 *About 450 cal, 28 g fat (9 g sat), 38 g pro, 450 mg sodium, 12 g carb, 4 g fiber*

Citrus-Marinated Steak and Crispy Potatoes

ACTIVE 15 MIN. | TOTAL 35 MIN.

INGREDIENTS

RED ONIONS
2 small, cut into ½-in. thick wedges

YELLOW POTATOES
1¼ lbs, cut into ¾-in.-thick wedges

CHIMICHURRI
½ cup

ORANGE
1

STRIP STEAK
2 12-oz strip steaks (each about 1½ in. thick), trimmed

1. Heat oven to 425°F. Brush a large rimmed baking sheet with **1 Tbsp olive oil**. Arrange red onions and yellow potatoes on baking sheet then season with **½ tsp each kosher salt and pepper**. Roast until golden brown and tender, 20 to 25 min.

2. Meanwhile, stir together chimichurri, 1 tsp orange zest and 3 Tbsp orange juice in a small bowl.

3. Transfer ⅓ cup orange chimichurri to pie plate, add strip steaks and turn to coat. Let marinate at least 10 min. and up to 30 min.

4. Heat **1 Tbsp oil** in a large cast-iron skillet on medium. Remove steaks from marinade and pat dry. Season with **¼ tsp each salt and pepper** and cook until browned, 4 min. Turn and cook 2 min. more, then transfer skillet to oven and roast to desired doneness, 2 to 4 min. for medium-rare. Transfer to cutting board and let rest at least 5 min. before slicing.

5. Serve with red onions, yellow potatoes, reserved orange chimichurri and orange wedges for squeezing.

SERVES 4 *About 495 cal, 20.5 g fat (7 g sat), 43 g pro, 580 mg sodium, 35 g carb, 3 g fiber*

Sheet Pan Asparagus Frittata

ACTIVE **15 MIN.** | TOTAL **40 MIN.**

INGREDIENTS

ASPARAGUS
1 lb

EGGS
12

MILK
1 cup

BABY SPINACH
2 cups, sliced

GOAT CHEESE
2½ oz, crumbled
(about ½ cup)

1. Heat oven to 375°F. Brush a large rimmed baking sheet with **1 tsp olive oil.** Trim, then slice asparagus ends on bias ¼ in. thick, leaving top 4 in. of each spear intact, then halve each spear tip lengthwise (or quarter if thick).

2. In large bowl, whisk together eggs, milk, **1 tsp kosher salt and ½ tsp pepper.**

3. Stir in baby spinach and bias-cut asparagus, then pour into prepared baking sheet. Scatter top with asparagus tips and goat cheese. Bake, rotating pan halfway through, until eggs are puffed and middle no longer jiggles, 20 to 22 min. Let rest 5 min. before slicing. Serve with **watercress** and **sliced red onion** tossed with olive oil and **lemon juice**, if desired.

SERVES 6 *About 220 cal, 14 g fat (6 g sat), 18 g pro, 592 mg sodium, 6 g carb, 2 g fiber*

BONUS IDEA	**Leftover Lunch:** *Serve extra frittata slices inside a split slice of focaccia, topped with sliced onions and greens.*

Ham and Brie Quesadillas

ACTIVE **15 MIN.** | TOTAL **15 MIN.**

INGREDIENTS

FLOUR TORTILLAS
2 large

**COUNTRY DIJON
MUSTARD**
4 tsp, plus more
for serving

CORNICHON
8, sliced, plus more
for serving

HAM
4 oz, sliced

BRIE
4 oz Brie, sliced

1. Heat broiler. Spread each flour tortilla with 2 tsp country Dijon mustard.

2. Sprinkle flour tortillas with cornichons. Layer ham and Brie on one side of each flour tortilla, then fold tops over into half-moons and place on large rimmed baking sheet. Broil until tops are golden brown and Brie has melted, about 2 minutes. Cut into wedges. Serve with additional cornichons and country Dijon mustard.

SERVES 4 *About 245 cal, 13 g fat (7 g sat), 14 g pro, 1080 mg sodium, 19 g carb, 1 g fiber*

Pea Pesto Pappardelle

ACTIVE 20 MIN. | TOTAL 25 MIN.

INGREDIENTS

PAPPARDELLE
12 oz

LEMON
1

FROZEN PEAS
1½ cups, thawed,
divided

RICOTTA
½ cup

PARMESAN
¼ cup grated

1. Cook pappardelle per pkg. directions. Finely grate 1 tsp lemon zest and set aside. Reserve ½ cup pasta cooking water, then drain pasta and return pasta to pot. Add 2 Tbsp lemon juice and toss.

2. While pasta is cooking, pulse 1 cup frozen peas in food processor to roughly chop.

3. Add ricotta, Parmesan and lemon zest to peas and pulse a few times. Season with **½ tsp kosher salt and ¼ tsp pepper**. Add pea mixture to pasta and toss to coat, adding reserved pasta water, 1 to 2 Tbsp at a time if it seems dry. Toss with remaining ½ cup whole frozen peas. Sprinkle with **chopped chives** if desired.

SERVES 4 *About 430 cal, 6.5 g fat (2.5 g sat), 19 g pro, 100 mg sodium, 70 g carb, 5 g fiber*

WEEK 6 DINNERS
Week-At-A-Glance

DAY 36
Apricot Grilled Pork
Tenderloin and Peppers

DAY 37
Summer Squash, Mint and
Pecorino Pasta

DAY 38
Sticky Grilled Chicken with
Corn and Potatoes

DAY 39
Waffle Nachos

DAY 40
Steak with Farro Salad and
Grilled Green Beans

DAY 41
Tomato and White Bean Soup

DAY 42
Shrimp Packets with
Kale and Couscous

NOTES

_____

_____

_____

_____

_____

Shopping List

PRODUCE

2	large cloves garlic
1	medium red onion
4	medium yellow potatoes
24	oz green beans
4	peppers (red, yellow, orange or a combination)
1½	lbs summer squash (zucchini and yellow squash)
2	medium zucchini
1	lb cocktail tomatoes
4	ears corn (in the husk)
1	5-oz container baby kale
½	cup basil
⅓	cup mint
1	lemon
1	lime

MEAT & SEAFOOD

1½	lbs skirt steak
2	small pork tenderloins (about ¾ lb each)
4	small chicken legs (about 2 lbs)
6	oz fully cooked andouille sausage
1	lb large peeled and deveined shrimp

REFRIGERATED & DAIRY

4	large eggs
4	oz Cheddar
3	oz pecorino
½	cup pico de gallo

FROZEN

8	frozen buttermilk waffles

PANTRY

12	oz rigatoni
1	8.8-oz pkg. quick-cooking farro
1	cup couscous
2	15.5-oz cans cannellini beans
1	24-oz jar marinara sauce (we used Rao's)
6	Tbsp sundried tomato pesto
2	Tbsp white wine vinegar
¼	cup apricot jam
¼	cup red pepper jelly
⅓	cup nutritional yeast

COOKING STAPLES

8½	Tbsp olive oil, plus more for serving
	Kosher salt and black pepper

BOOST IT

Some recipes this week may call for these flavor boosters and we highly recommend sprinkling them in if you already have them on hand. If you don't, it's OK—all the recipes are great on their own!

- Fresh cilantro
- Baguette

Apricot Grilled Pork Tenderloin and Peppers

ACTIVE **25 MIN.** | TOTAL **30 MIN.**

INGREDIENTS

PEPPERS
4 (red, yellow, orange or a combination), quartered

RED ONION
1 medium, cut into ½-in.-thick wedges

PORK TENDERLOIN
2 small (about ¾ lb each)

APRICOT JAM
¼ cup

WHITE WINE VINEGAR
2 Tbsp

1. Heat grill to medium high. Toss peppers and onion with **1 Tbsp olive oil** in a large bowl; season with **¼ tsp each kosher salt and pepper**.

2. Season pork tenderloins with **¼ tsp each salt and pepper**. Grill vegetables and pork, covered, turning occasionally, until vegetables are tender, 8 to 10 min. Transfer vegetables to cutting board.

3. Meanwhile, mix apricot jam and white wine vinegar in a small bowl. Continue grilling pork, basting with sauce, until cooked through and thermometer registers 145°F when inserted into thickest part, 3 to 6 min. more. Let rest 5 min. before slicing.

4. Coarsely chop peppers and serve with onion, pork and any remaining sauce.

SERVES 4 *About 320 cal, 9 g fat (2.5 g sat), 36 g pro, 335 mg sodium, 23 g carb, 3 g fiber*

Summer Squash, Mint and Pecorino Pasta

ACTIVE **10 MIN.** | TOTAL **25 MIN.**

INGREDIENTS

RIGATONI
12 oz rigatoni

SUMMER SQUASH
1½ lbs (zucchini and
yellow squash), thinly
sliced into half moons

PECORINO
3 oz, grated, plus more
for serving

MINT
⅓ cup, thinly sliced

LEMON
1 Tbsp fresh juice

1. Cook rigatoni per pkg. directions. Reserve ¾ cup pasta cooking water, then drain pasta.

2. Meanwhile, heat **2 Tbsp olive oil** in a large deep skillet on medium. Add summer squash and **½ tsp each kosher salt and pepper** and cook, tossing occasionally, until very tender but still holds its shape, 10 to 12 min.

3. Add rigatoni and pecorino to skillet and toss, adding reserved pasta water, 2 Tbsp at a time, to form a sauce that coats pasta. Add rigatoni and pecorino to skillet and cook, tossing and adding reserved pasta water 2 Tbsp at a time as needed, until rigatoni has absorbed most of liquid and is coated with a glossy sauce, about 2 min.

4. Fold in mint and lemon juice. Top with additional pecorino and **pepper**.

SERVES 4 *About 490 cal, 13.5 g fat (5 g sat), 21 g pro, 505 mg sodium, 71 g carb, 5 g fiber*

Sticky Grilled Chicken with Corn and Potatoes

ACTIVE **40 MIN.** | TOTAL **40 MIN.**

INGREDIENTS

RED PEPPER JELLY
¼ cup

LIME JUICE
½ Tbsp

CHICKEN LEGS
4 small (2 lbs total),
split into 4 thighs and
4 drumsticks

YELLOW POTATOES
4 medium

CORN
4 ears

1. Heat grill to medium. In small bowl, stir together red pepper jelly and lime juice.

2. Season chicken legs with **½ tsp each kosher salt and pepper**. Grill, covered, turning occasionally, 20 min. Uncover and continue grilling, basting with sauce, until chicken is cooked through, 5 to 7 min. more.

3. While chicken is grilling for first 20 min., prick potatoes all over with fork and microwave on high on large plate, flipping halfway through, until barely tender, 4 to 5 min. When cool enough to handle, slice lengthwise into ¾-in.-thick planks. Brush potatoes with **2 Tbsp olive oil** and season with **¼ tsp each salt and pepper**. Grill uncovered along with chicken until charred and tender, 3 to 4 min. per side.

4. Meanwhile, microwave corn for 10 min. Carefully remove from microwave using kitchen towel or mitts. When cool enough to handle, slice off bottom end from each ear, including a bit of the cob. Squeeze out each corn cob then discard husk. Cut corn into thirds (or quarters if large) and serve with chicken and potatoes. Top with **cilantro** to add fresh flavor (and a pop of color) if desired.

SERVES 4 *About 515 cal, 18.5 g fat (4 g sat), 34 g pro, 540 mg sodium, 58 g carb, 5 g fiber*

Waffle Nachos

ACTIVE 15 MIN. | **TOTAL 15 MIN.**

INGREDIENTS

BUTTERMILK WAFFLES
8 frozen

ANDOUILLE SAUSAGE
6 oz, fully cooked, sliced ¼ in. thick

EGGS
4 large, beaten

CHEDDAR
4 oz, coarsely grated (about 1¼ cups)

PICO DE GALLO
½ cup, drained

1. Cook waffles per pkg. directions. Transfer to cutting board and cut into wedges. Heat oven to 450°F and line large rimmed baking sheet with parchment paper. Arrange waffles on top.

2. Heat **1 tsp olive oil** in a medium nonstick skillet on medium. Add andouille sausage and cook until browned, 2 to 3 min. per side. Transfer to plate.

3. Wipe out skillet and heat **2 tsp oil** on medium. Add eggs and cook, stirring often, until eggs begin to set. Season with **¼ tsp each kosher salt and pepper**.

4. Scatter sausage, eggs and Cheddar over waffles and roast until Cheddar melts, about 2 min. Spoon pico de gallo over top and sprinkle with **cilantro** if desired.

SERVES 4 *About 624 cal, 40 g fat (15 g sat), 28 g pro, 1520 mg sodium, 37 g carb, 2 g fiber*

BONUS IDEA	**Quick Stew:** *Thinly slice leftover andouille sausage and brown in oil in a saucepan. Then stir in chicken broth and canned white beans and bring to a simmer. Stir in baby spinach or kale and cook until just wilted. Serve topped with grated Parmesan.*

Steak with Farro Salad and Grilled Green Beans

ACTIVE 20 MIN. | **TOTAL 25 MIN.**

INGREDIENTS

FARRO
1 8.8-oz pkg.
quick-cooking

SKIRT STEAK
1½ lbs, cut crosswise
into 4-in. pieces

GREEN BEANS
12 oz, trimmed

**SUNDRIED
TOMATO PESTO**
6 Tbsp

BASIL
½ cup, chopped

1. Cook farro per pkg. directions. Drain and transfer to large bowl.

2. Meanwhile, heat grill or grill pan to medium-high. Season skirt steak with **½ tsp each kosher salt and pepper**. Grill skirt steak to desired doneness, 2 to 4 min. per side for medium-rare, depending on thickness. Transfer to cutting board and let rest at least 5 min. before slicing.

3. Toss green beans with **½ Tbsp olive oil** and **¼ tsp each salt and pepper** in a large bowl. Grill beans along with steak, turning occasionally, until charred and just tender, 2 to 4 min.

4. To farro, stir in sundried tomato pesto, basil and a **pinch of salt**. Divide farro salad and green beans among plates and top with steak.

SERVES 4 *About 680 cal, 29.5 g fat (8.5 g sat), 47 g pro, 610 mg sodium, 6 g fiber*

Tomato and White Bean Soup

ACTIVE **20 MIN.** | TOTAL **25 MIN.**

INGREDIENTS

MARINARA SAUCE
1 24-oz jar (we used Rao's)

NUTRITIONAL YEAST
⅓ cup

GREEN BEANS
12 oz, trimmed and cut on bias into thirds or fourths if large

CANNELLINI BEANS
2 15.5-oz cans, rinsed

ZUCCHINI
2 medium (about 8 oz each), trimmed and quartered lengthwise, then sliced into ¼-in. pieces

1. To blender, add half the marinara, the nutritional yeast and **3 cups water** and blend on high to combine, 30 seconds. Transfer to large pot and repeat with remaining marinara and **3 cups water**.

2. Bring marinara mixture to a simmer. Stir in green beans and cannellini beans and simmer 3 min.

3. Add zucchini and simmer until vegetables are just tender, 1 to 2 min more. Taste and season with **½ tsp kosher salt** if needed. Top with **cracked pepper** and a drizzle of **olive oil**. Serve with **baguette slices** if desired.

SERVES **4 to 6** *About 350 cal, 12 g fat (2 g sat), 18 g pro, 610 mg sodium, 44 g carb, 12 g fiber*

Shrimp Packets with Kale and Couscous

ACTIVE **10 MIN.** | TOTAL **25 MIN.**

INGREDIENTS

COUSCOUS
1 cup

BABY KALE
1 5-oz container

COCKTAIL TOMATOES
1 lb, quartered

GARLIC
2 large cloves, thinly sliced

SHRIMP
1 lb large peeled and deveined

1. Heat grill to medium-high. Cut eight 12-in. squares of foil. In medium bowl, combine couscous with **½ cup water**.

2. Divide kale among 4 squares of foil. Top with couscous, then tomatoes and garlic.

3. Top tomatoes with shrimp, drizzle with **2 Tbsp olive oil** and season with **¼ tsp each kosher salt and pepper**. Cover shrimp with another piece of foil; fold each edge up and over 3 times, tucking underneath to seal.

4. Grill, covered, 15 min. Transfer packets to plates. Watching out for steam, very carefully cut an "X" in center of each packet and fold back triangles to serve.

SERVES 4 *About 335 cal, 9 g fat (1 g sat), 41 g pro, 795 mg sodium, 41 g carb, 5 g fiber*

WEEK 7 DINNERS
Week-At-A-Glance

DAY 43
Sheet Pan Chicken Fajitas

DAY 44
Grilled Pork with
Smoky Corn Salad

DAY 45
Skillet Pesto
Chicken and Beans

DAY 46
Grilled Lamb and
Artichoke Kebabs

DAY 47
Cumin-Lime Shrimp

DAY 48
Creamy Corn Pasta

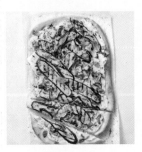

DAY 49
Grilled Leek, Zucchini
and Ricotta Pizza

NOTES

WEEK 7
Shopping List

PRODUCE

1	yellow onion
2	peppers (red and yellow)
2	large zucchini
1	large leek
8	oz green beans
10	ears corn
1	cup cherry tomatoes
2½	bunches scallions
1	5-oz pkg. baby arugula
½	cup basil
¼	cup mint
2	Tbsp cilantro
½	small pineapple
2	lemons
2	limes

MEAT & SEAFOOD

4	6-oz boneless, skinless chicken breasts
8	small chicken thighs (about 2 lbs)
1¼	lbs pork tenderloin
1¼	lbs boneless lamb leg
1	lb large peeled and deveined shrimp

REFRIGERATED & DAIRY

1	lb pizza dough
1	oz Romano
2	cups ricotta

PANTRY

12	oz orecchiette
1	cup long grain white rice
1	15-oz can butter beans
2	Tbsp adobo sauce
5	Tbsp chipotle mayonnaise
2	Tbsp pesto
8	large marinated artichokes
⅛	tsp ground cumin

COOKING STAPLES

2	Tbsp unsalted butter
6	Tbsp olive oil, plus more for serving
	Kosher salt and black pepper

BOOST IT

Some recipes this week may call for these flavor boosters and we highly recommend sprinkling them in if you already have them on hand. If you don't, it's OK—all the recipes are great on their own!

- Lime
- Tortillas
- Fresh cilantro
- Grated Parmesan
- Basil
- Crumbled feta
- Hot sauce

Sheet Pan Chicken Fajitas

ACTIVE **20 MIN.** | TOTAL **40 MIN.**

INGREDIENTS

CHICKEN BREASTS
4 6-oz boneless, skinless
chicken breasts

ADOBO SAUCE
2 Tbsp

PEPPERS
2 (red and yellow), sliced

YELLOW ONION
1, sliced

PINEAPPLE
½ small, cut into
matchsticks

1. Heat broiler. In medium bowl, toss chicken breasts with adobo sauce and **¼ tsp kosher salt**. Place on large rimmed baking sheet and broil 6 min.; transfer to plate. Reduce oven temp to 425°F.

2. On same baking sheet, toss peppers, onion and pineapple with **1 Tbsp olive oil** and **¼ tsp salt**. Roast 15 min.

3. Nestle chicken breasts among vegetables and roast until chicken breasts are cooked through and vegetables are tender, about 5 min. more. Slice chicken and serve with vegetables. Add a **squeeze of lime** for brightness and serve with **warmed tortillas** if desired.

SERVES 4 *About 310 cal, 10 g fat (2 g sat), 36 g pro, 355 mg sodium, 19 g carb, 3 g fiber*

BONUS IDEA	**Next-Day Breakfast:** *Slice up your leftover pineapple, then broil until golden brown and caramelized. Pile on top of pancakes or waffles, then sprinkle with toasted coconut or add a dollop of coconut yogurt.*

Grilled Pork with Smoky Corn Salad

ACTIVE 30 MIN. | TOTAL **30 MIN.**

INGREDIENTS

CORN
4 ears, shucked

SCALLION
1 bunch, trimmed

**CHIPOTLE
MAYONNAISE**
5 Tbsp, divided

**PORK
TENDERLOIN**
1¼ lbs

1. Heat grill to medium. Brush corn and scallions with **1 Tbsp olive oil**; season with ¼ tsp **each kosher salt and pepper**. Put 3 Tbsp chipotle mayonnaise in large bowl and 2 Tbsp in small bowl and set aside.

2. Grill corn and scallions, covered, turning occasionally, until tender and charred, 2 to 3 min. for scallions and 8 to 10 min. for corn. Transfer to cutting board and let rest until cool enough to handle.

3. Meanwhile, trim and cut pork tenderloin crosswise into 8 pieces. Pound each piece to ¼ in. thick. Season with **¼ tsp each salt and pepper** and grill, covered, until pork is almost cooked through, about 2 min. Flip, brush with 1 Tbsp chipotle mayonnaise from small bowl and cook until grill marks appear, 1 to 2 min. more. Flip and brush with remaining 1 Tbsp chipotle mayo; grill until cooked through, 30 sec. to 1 min.

4. To large bowl with chipotle mayonnaise, add 1 tsp lime zest, 1 Tbsp lime juice, 1 Tbsp water and **¼ tsp each salt and pepper** and whisk to combine.

5. Slice scallions into 1-in. pieces and cut kernels from corn cobs; add to dressing and stir to combine. Serve with pork and lime wedges. Sprinkle with **chopped cilantro** if desired.

SERVES 4 *About 410 cal, 22 g fat (4 g sat), 32 g pro, 550 mg sodium, 24 g carb, 3 g fiber*

Skillet Pesto Chicken and Beans

ACTIVE **20 MIN.** | TOTAL **25 MIN.**

INGREDIENTS

CHICKEN THIGHS
8 small (about 2 lbs)

GREEN BEANS
8 oz, halved

CHERRY TOMATOES
1 cup

BUTTER BEANS
1 15-oz can, rinsed

PESTO
2 Tbsp

1. Heat oven to 425°F. Season chicken thighs with ½ tsp each **kosher salt and pepper**. Heat **1 Tbsp olive oil** in a large ovenproof skillet on medium-high. Add chicken thighs and cook, skin sides down, until golden brown, about 6 min.

2. Turn chicken thighs over, add green beans, tomatoes and butter beans and season with **¼ tsp salt**. Transfer skillet to oven and roast until chicken thighs are cooked through, 12 to 15 min.

3. Brush pesto over chicken thighs. Top with **grated Parmesan** and **chopped basil** — both ingredients are typically found in pesto — if desired.

SERVES 4 *About 450 cal, 26 g fat (6.5 g sat), 38 g pro, 770 mg sodium, 22 g carb, 6 g fiber*

BONUS IDEA	**Easy Breakfast:** *On small rimmed baking sheet, toss any leftover tomatoes with olive oil and a pinch each smoked paprika, salt and pepper and roast at 400°F until tomatoes begin to until burst. Refrigerate overnight then spoon over cottage cheese or cream cheese toast.*

Grilled Lamb and Artichoke Kebabs

ACTIVE **25 MIN.** | TOTAL **30 MIN.**

INGREDIENTS

LAMB LEG
1¼ lbs boneless, trimmed
and cut into 1-in. pieces

LEMON
2

ARTICHOKES
8 large marinated, halved

SCALLIONS
1 bunch, cut into
2-in. pieces

BABY ARUGULA
1 5-oz pkg.

1. Toss lamb with **1 Tbsp olive oil** and **½ tsp each kosher salt and pepper** in a medium bowl. Grate zest of lemons over lamb and toss to coat. Cut lemons in half and set aside.

2. Thread lamb, marinated artichokes and scallions onto skewers.

3. Heat grill or grill pan to medium-high. Grill kebabs, turning occasionally, until lamb reaches desired doneness, 6 to 8 min. for medium-rare. Grill lemons cut sides down until charred, 2 to 3 min. Squeeze 1 lemon half over kebabs.

4. Toss baby arugula with **1 Tbsp oil**, juice of 1 lemon half and **¼ tsp each salt and pepper** in a large bowl. Serve with kebabs and remaining lemon halves for squeezing. Sprinkle arugula salad with **crumbled feta** if desired.

SERVES 4 *About 310 cal, 18.5 g fat (4.5 g sat), 29 g pro, 625 mg sodium, 7 g carb, 3 g fiber*

Cumin-Lime Shrimp

ACTIVE 15 MIN. | **TOTAL 15 MIN.**

INGREDIENTS

WHITE RICE
1 cup long grain

CUMIN
⅛ tsp ground

LIME
1

SHRIMP
1 lb large peeled
and deveined

CILANTRO
2 Tbsp

1. Cook rice per pkg. directions.

2. Combine **2 Tbsp unsalted butter** (at room temp) with ground cumin, ¼ tsp lime zest and **pinch kosher salt** in a medium bowl, mashing until combined. Set aside.

3. Heat **1 Tbsp olive oil** in a large cast-iron skillet on medium. Add shrimp in single layer and cook until golden brown on both sides and opaque throughout, 2 to 3 min. per side.

4. Remove skillet from heat. Add cumin-lime butter and cilantro, then stir until butter melts. Cut lime into wedges and serve with cumin-lime shrimp and cooked rice.

SERVES 4 *About 168 cal, 9.5 g fat (4 g sat), 20 g pro, 152 mg sodium, 1 g carb, 0 g fiber*

Creamy Corn Pasta

ACTIVE **20 MIN.** | TOTAL **20 MIN.**

INGREDIENTS

CORN
6 ears, shucked

ORECCHIETTE
12 oz

ROMANO
1 oz, finely grated, plus
more for serving

SCALLIONS
2, chopped

BASIL
½ cup, plus more
for serving

1. Bring large pot of water to a boil. Add a generous pinch **kosher salt**. Add corn and cook 2 min. Transfer to cutting board.

2. Add orecchiette to same pot and cook per pkg. directions. Reserve 1 cup pasta cooking water, then drain pasta and return to pot.

3. When corn is cool enough to handle but while pasta is still cooking, cut off kernels (you should have about 3 cups). Transfer 2 cups to blender along with Romano, ¾ cup reserved pasta water and ¼ tsp salt; puree until very smooth.

4. Toss pasta with corn puree, adding some reserved pasta water, 1 Tbsp at a time, if pasta seems dry. Fold in scallions, basil and reserved corn. Serve sprinkled with additional Romano and basil, as well as **hot sauce** if desired.

SERVES 4 *About 484 cal, 5 g fat (2 g sat), 19 g pro, 402 mg sodium, 96 g carb, 5 g fiber*

BONUS IDEA	**Leftover Lunch:** *Make use of the orecchiette left behind in the box. Cook it, then toss with grape tomatoes (quartered), basil (chopped), a pinch salt, splash of balsamic vinegar and a drizzle of olive oil. Add bocconcini or chopped mozzarella, chopped salami or extra cooked corn, if you have it. Stash in the fridge until you're ready to eat.*

Grilled Leek, Zucchini and Ricotta Pizza

ACTIVE **25 MIN.** | TOTAL **45 MIN.**

INGREDIENTS

PIZZA DOUGH
1 lb

LEEK
1 large, white and light
green parts only, halved
lengthwise

ZUCCHINI
2 large, trimmed
and sliced lengthwise
into planks

RICOTTA
2 cups

MINT
¼ cup small fresh
mint leaves

1. Heat oven to 425°F and heat grill to medium-high. Line large rimmed baking sheet with parchment paper. Shape pizza dough into large rectangle, then transfer to prepared baking sheet and bake 10 min. Remove pizza crust from oven and increase oven to 475°F.

2. Brush leek and zucchini with olive oil and season with **kosher salt and pepper**. Grill leek and zucchini, turning leek occasionally and zucchini once, until tender, 5 to 8 min. Thinly slice leek.

3. Mix ricotta with **½ tsp salt**. Spread on pizza crust. Top with vegetables. Bake until browned, 5 to 8 min. Drizzle with oil and sprinkle with mint.

SERVES *4* *About 575 cal, 26.5 g fat (11.5 g sat), 22 g pro, 1,235 mg sodium, 60 g carb, 4 g fiber*

WEEK 8 DINNERS
Week-At-A-Glance

DAY 50
Balsamic Chicken Caprese

DAY 51
Sesame-Crusted Salmon with
Miso Butter Radishes

DAY 52
Chorizo-Stuffed Zucchini

DAY 53
Paprika Chicken with Crispy
Chickpeas and Tomatoes

DAY 54
Shrimp and Sweet Corn "Grits"

DAY 55
Pork, Pineapple and
Onion Skewers

DAY 56
Creamy Kale Pasta

NOTES

_____

_____

_____

_____

WEEK 8
Shopping List

PRODUCE
8   cloves garlic
1   small red onion
8   oz baby peppers
4   zucchini
1   vine-ripe or heirloom tomato
12   oz cherry tomatoes
10   ears corn
1½   lbs small radishes, including leaves
6   cups baby kale
4   scallions
¼   cup basil
½   cup cilantro
½   small fresh pineapple

MEAT & SEAFOOD
8   6-oz boneless, skinless chicken breasts
1   lb pork loin
2   small links fresh Mexican chorizo (about 6 oz total)
2   slices bacon
4   6-oz skinless salmon fillets
20   large peeled and deveined shrimp (about 12 oz)

REFRIGERATED & DAIRY
6   oz mozzarella
3   oz Monterey Jack cheese
⅓   cup grated Parmesan
½   cup cottage cheese
1½   Tbsp white miso

PANTRY
12   oz short pasta (like orecchiette or gemelli)
1   cup long grain white rice
1   15-oz can chickpeas
¼   cup balsamic vinegar
¼   cup teriyaki sauce
4   tsp sesame seeds
2   tsp paprika
⅛   tsp smoked paprika

COOKING STAPLES
1½   Tbsp unsalted butter
1   8-oz bottle olive oil
    Kosher salt and black pepper

BOOST IT

Some recipes this week may call for these flavor boosters and we highly recommend sprinkling them in if you already have them on hand. If you don't, it's OK—all the recipes are great on their own!

- Jalapeños

Balsamic Chicken Caprese

ACTIVE 15 MIN. | **TOTAL 30 MIN.**

INGREDIENTS

CHICKEN BREASTS
4 6-oz boneless,
skinless chicken breasts
(1½ lbs total)

BALSAMIC VINEGAR
¼ cup

MOZZARELLA
6 oz fresh, sliced

BASIL
¼ cup basil

HEIRLOOM TOMATO
1, sliced ¼ in. thick

1. Heat oven to 400°F. Heat **1 Tbsp olive oil** in a large ovenproof skillet on medium-high. Season chicken breasts with **½ tsp kosher salt and ¼ tsp pepper** and cook until deep golden brown on one side, 4 to 5 min.

2. Flip chicken breasts and cook 1 min. Reduce heat to medium, add balsamic vinegar and gently simmer until slightly thickened and syrupy, 1 to 2 min. Transfer skillet to oven and roast 10 min.

3. Turn chicken breasts to coat in vinegar, top with mozzarella and roast until chicken breasts are cooked through and mozzarella begins to melt, about 2 min.

4. Serve topped with basil and tomato. Sprinkle with **salt and pepper** and drizzle with any balsamic glaze from skillet.

SERVES 4 *About 376 cal, 17 g fat (7 g sat), 48 g pro, 489 mg sodium, 6 g carb, 0 g fiber*

BONUS IDEA	**Leftover Lunch:** *Feature any extra chicken, tomatoes or mozzarella in a chopped salad. Cut everything into small pieces, then toss with chopped lettuce and cannellini beans. Add a drizzle of balsamic and olive oil.*

Sesame-Crusted Salmon with Miso Butter Radishes

ACTIVE **20 MIN.** | TOTAL **30 MIN.**

INGREDIENTS

WHITE RICE
1 cup long grain

RADISHES
1½ lbs small, including leaves

WHITE MISO
1½ Tbsp

SALMON
4 6-oz skinless fillets

SESAME SEEDS
4 tsp

1. Heat oven to 450°F. Cook rice per pkg. directions.

2. Meanwhile, trim and halve radishes; wash and reserve leaves. Coat a large rimmed baking sheet with **1 Tbsp olive oil**. Arrange radishes, cut sides down, on baking sheet and drizzle with **½ Tbsp oil**. Roast 12 min.

3. Meanwhile, combine **1½ Tbsp unsalted butter** (at room temp) and white miso in a large bowl.

4. Season salmon fillets with **¼ tsp pepper**, then sprinkle with sesame seeds, pressing to adhere. Nestle salmon among radishes, reduce oven temperature to 425°F and roast until salmon is just opaque throughout and radishes are golden brown, 10 to 12 min. Transfer salmon to plates.

5. Transfer radishes to bowl with miso butter (leaving behind any oil). Toss to coat, then fold in 3 cups radish leaves until beginning to wilt. Serve with salmon and rice.

SERVES 4 *About 510 cal, 14.5 g fat (5 g sat), 40 g pro, 390 mg sodium, 51 g carb, 4 g fiber*

BONUS IDEA	**Leftover Lunch:** *Very thinly slice extra raw radishes to make a light-and-bright radish salad. Serve with your go-to protein (leftover salmon, perhaps?).*

Chorizo-Stuffed Zucchini

ACTIVE 20 MIN. | TOTAL 35 MIN.

INGREDIENTS

ZUCCHINI
4 (about 6 oz each)

MEXICAN CHORIZO
2 small links fresh
(about 6 oz total),
casings discarded,
meat crumbled into
small pieces

SCALLIONS
2, thinly sliced

**MONTEREY JACK
CHEESE**
3 oz, coarsely grated

CILANTRO
½ cup, chopped, plus
more for serving

1. Place large rimmed baking sheet in oven and heat to 450°F. Cut zucchini in half lengthwise and, using teaspoon, hollow out each zucchini half. Brush cut sides with **1 tsp olive oil**, then carefully arrange zucchini, cut sides down, on preheated baking sheet. Roast 5 min.

2. Meanwhile, heat **2 tsp oil** in a large skillet on medium-high. Add Mexican chorizo and cook, breaking up into pieces with wooden spoon, until no longer pink, 3 to 4 min. Using slotted spoon, transfer to bowl.

3. Add scallions to Mexican chorizo and toss to combine. Fold in Monterey Jack cheese and cilantro.

4. Turn zucchini cut sides up and season with **¼ tsp each kosher salt and pepper**. Divide chorizo mixture among zucchini halves (about ¼ cup per half) and roast until zucchini are just tender, 8 to 10 min. more. Sprinkle with cilantro.

SERVES 4 *About 250 cal, 19 g fat (8 g sat), 14 g pro, 560 mg sodium, 5 g carb, 2 g fiber*

BONUS IDEA	**Next-Day Breakfast:** *Cook extra chorizo in a skillet, breaking into pieces, then toss with roasted vegetables. Top with a fried egg and some cilantro.*

Paprika Chicken with Crispy Chickpeas and Tomatoes

ACTIVE **15 MIN.** | TOTAL **20 MIN.**

INGREDIENTS

CHERRY TOMATOES
12 oz

GARLIC
8 cloves, smashed in
their skins

CHICKPEAS
1 15-oz can, rinsed

CHICKEN BREASTS
4 6-oz boneless, skinless
chicken breasts

PAPRIKA
2 tsp

1. Heat oven to 425°F. Toss tomatoes, garlic and chickpeas with **2 Tbsp olive oil** and **¼ tsp each kosher salt and pepper** on a large rimmed baking sheet. Roast 10 min.

2. Heat **1 Tbsp oil** in a large skillet on medium. Season chicken breasts with paprika and **½ tsp each salt and pepper** and cook until golden brown on one side, 5 to 6 min. Flip and cook 1 min. more.

3. Transfer chicken breasts to baking sheet with tomatoes and chickpeas and roast until cooked through, about 6 min. more. Before serving, discard garlic skins.

SERVES **4** *About 390 cal, 16 g fat (2.5 g sat), 40 g pro, 590 mg sodium, 21 g carb, 6 g fiber*

BONUS IDEA	**Leftover Lunch:** *Wrap up any leftovers in a warmed pita and top with a spoonful of Greek yogurt or labneh.*

Shrimp and Sweet Corn "Grits"

ACTIVE **25 MIN.** | TOTAL **25 MIN.**

INGREDIENTS

CORN
10 ears

BACON
2 slices, cut into
½-in. pieces

BASIL
¼ cup, roughly chopped,
plus more for serving

SHRIMP
20 large peeled and
deveined (about 12 oz),
patted dry

SMOKED PAPRIKA
⅛ tsp

1. Cut kernels from corn to total 6 cups. In food processor, pulse half of kernels until almost smooth. Add remaining kernels and pulse twice to just combine.

2. In large skillet, cook bacon on medium, stirring occasionally, until crisp, 5 to 6 min.; transfer to plate.

3. Wipe out skillet and heat **1 Tbsp olive oil** on medium. Add corn mixture and **½ tsp each kosher salt and pepper** and cook, stirring occasionally, until just heated through, about 3 min. Fold in bacon and basil.

4. In second large skillet, heat **1 Tbsp oil** on medium-high. Season shrimp with smoked paprika and **½ tsp each salt and pepper**; cook in single layer until golden brown and opaque throughout, 1 to 2 min. per side. Serve with corn "grits" and sprinkle with additional basil.

SERVES 4 *About 347 cal, 12 g fat (2.5 g sat), 26 g pro, 695 mg sodium, 41 g carb, 5 g fiber*

BONUS IDEA	**Next-Day Breakfast:** *Crisp up leftover bacon and saute leftover shrimp until opaque throughout. Toss shrimp and bacon with chopped tomatoes, then spoon into lettuce leaves and squirt of mayo for a shrimp BLT.*

Pork, Pineapple and Onion Skewers

ACTIVE 30 MIN. | TOTAL 45 MIN.

INGREDIENTS

PORK LOIN
1 lb, trimmed and cut into
1-in. pieces

BABY PEPPERS
8 oz, cut into 1-in. pieces

RED ONION
1 small, cut into
6 wedges, then
halved crosswise

FRESH PINEAPPLE
½ small, cut into 1-in.
chunks (about 2 cups)

TERIYAKI SAUCE
¼ cup, plus more
for serving

1. Heat grill to medium. Toss pork loin, baby peppers, red onion and pineapple with **2 Tbsp olive oil** and **½ tsp each kosher salt and pepper** in a large bowl. Thread onto skewers.

2. Grill skewers, turning occasionally, and basting with teriyaki sauce during the last 5 min. of cooking, until pork is cooked through, 8 to 10 min.

3. Serve with additional teriyaki sauce. Top skewers with **sliced jalapeños** right before serving to dial up the heat if desired.

SERVES 4 *About 310 cal, 11 g fat (2.5 g sat), 29 g pro, 895 mg sodium, 24 g carb, 2 g fiber*

BONUS IDEA	**Leftover Lunch:** *Use teriyaki to marinate chicken or tofu before grilling, then assemble a quick sandwich by piling the protein onto a bun along with grilled pineapple slices.*

Creamy Kale Pasta

ACTIVE 25 MIN. | **TOTAL 25 MIN.**

INGREDIENTS

SHORT PASTA
12 oz (like orecchiette or gemelli)

SCALLIONS
2, roughly chopped

BABY KALE
6 cups, divided

COTTAGE CHEESE
½ cup

PARMESAN
⅓ cup grated, plus more for serving

1. Cook pasta per pkg. directions. Reserve ½ cup pasta cooking water, then drain and return pasta to pot.

2. While pasta cooks, pulse scallions and 3 cups baby kale in food processor to finely chop. Add cottage cheese, Parmesan and **½ tsp each kosher salt and pepper** and pulse to combine. Scrape down sides; then, with machine running, gradually add 2 **Tbsp olive oil** and puree until smooth.

3. Toss pasta with sauce to coat, then toss with remaining 3 cups baby kale, adding a couple of Tbsp of reserved pasta water as necessary to help kale wilt. Serve topped with **cracked pepper** and additional Parmesan.

SERVES 4 *About 445 cal, 11.5 g fat (3.5 g sat), 17 g pro, 464 mg sodium,67 g carb, 5 g fiber*

BONUS IDEA	**Next-Day Breakfast:** *Top toast with cottage cheese and fresh fruit (pineapples, berries, you name it). Drizzle with honey if desired.*

WEEK 9 DINNERS
Week-At-A-Glance

DAY 57
Air Fryer Salmon
and Swiss Chard

DAY 58
Roasted Cherry Chicken with
Parmesan Brussels Sprouts

DAY 59
Seared Steak with Blistered
Tomatoes and Green Beans

DAY 60
Jammy Grilled Cheese

DAY 61
Roasted Sausage and
Grapes with Polenta

DAY 62
Cauliflower Alfredo

DAY 63
Bacon, Egg and
Cheese Stackers

NOTES

_____

_____

_____

_____

WEEK 9
Shopping List

PRODUCE
3   cloves garlic
1   medium red onion
1   small red onion
1   yellow onion
4   small shallots
8   oz cauliflower
1¼   lbs Brussels sprouts
1   lb green beans
1   large bunch Swiss chard
1½   cups Tuscan kale
2   pints cherry or
     grape tomatoes
2   Tbsp fresh rosemary
1½   lbs seedless red grapes

MEAT & SEAFOOD
2   1½-in.-thick strip steaks
     (about 12oz each)
4   6-oz boneless, skinless
     chicken breasts
6   small links sweet Italian
     sausage (about 1¼ lbs)
4   slices bacon
4   5-oz salmon fillets

REFRIGERATED & DAIRY
4   large eggs
8   oz Brie
¼   cup coarsely grated extra
     sharp Cheddar
½   cup grated Parmesan

FROZEN
2   hash brown patties

BREAD & BAKERY
8   slices sourdough bread
4   8-in. flour tortillas

PANTRY
12   oz fettucine
1   cup instant polenta
2   Tbsp white wine vinegar
3   to 4 Tbsp lemon vinaigrette
2   Tbsp chili oil
½   cup jam (any flavor)
¾   cup dried cherries
1   Tbsp nutritional yeast

COOKING STAPLES
4   Tbsp softened
     unsalted butter
1   8-oz bottle olive oil
     Kosher salt and black pepper

BOOST IT

Some recipes this week may call for these flavor boosters and we highly recommend sprinkling them in if you already have them on hand. If you don't, it's OK—all the recipes are great on their own!

- Hot sauce
- Salad greens

Air Fryer Salmon and Swiss Chard

ACTIVE **25 MIN.** | TOTAL **25 MIN.**

INGREDIENTS

RED ONION
1 medium, cut into ½-in.-thick wedges

SWISS CHARD
1 large bunch, thick stems discarded, leaves chopped

GARLIC
2 cloves, sliced

SALMON
4 5-oz salmon fillets

CHILI OIL
For serving

1. Heat air fryer to 385°F. In a bowl, toss red onion with **½ Tbsp olive oil** and a **pinch each of kosher salt and pepper** and air-fry 5 min.

2. Toss red onion with Swiss chard, garlic, **1 Tbsp oil** and **¼ tsp each salt and pepper** and air-fry until Swiss chard and onion are just tender, about 5 min. more. Transfer to plates.

3. Increase air fryer to 400°F. Season salmon fillets with **½ tsp each salt and pepper** and air-fry until skin is crispy and salmon is opaque throughout, 8 to 10 min. Serve with vegetables and drizzle with chili oil.

SERVES 4 *About 243 cal, 10.5 g fat (2 g sat), 30 g pro, 641 mg sodium, 7 g carb, 2 g fiber*

Roasted Cherry Chicken with Parmesan Brussels Sprouts

ACTIVE **25 MIN.** | TOTAL **30 MIN.**

INGREDIENTS

CHICKEN BREASTS
4 6-oz boneless, skinless
chicken breasts

CHERRIES
¾ cup dried

BRUSSELS SPROUTS
1¼ lbs (about 20), halved

PARMESAN
½ cup grated

TUSCAN KALE
1½ cups, torn

1. Heat oven to 450°F. Heat **1 Tbsp olive oil** in a large ovenproof skillet on medium high. Season chicken breasts with **¼ tsp each kosher salt and pepper** and cook until deep golden brown, 6 to 8 min. Flip and cook 1 min. more.

2. Add dried cherries and **½ cup water** to skillet, then transfer to oven and roast until chicken breasts are cooked through, 6 to 7 min.

3. While chicken breasts are searing, line a large rimmed baking sheet with parchment paper, then coat it with **2 Tbsp oil**. Add Brussels sprouts, season with **½ tsp each salt and pepper**, arrange cut sides down and roast 8 min.

4. Drop 8 clumps (about 1 Tbsp each) of grated Parmesan into open spaces between sprouts and roast 4 min.

5. Massage kale with **2 tsp oil** in a medium bowl. Add to Brussels sprouts and roast 3 min. more. Serve vegetables with chicken breasts and cherries.

SERVES 4 *About 500 cal, 21.5 g fat (4 g sat), 47 g pro, 675 mg sodium, 32 g carb, 7 g fiber*

Seared Steak with Blistered Tomatoes and Green Beans

ACTIVE **25 MIN.** | TOTAL **25 MIN.**

INGREDIENTS

GREEN BEANS
1 lb, trimmed

CHERRY OR GRAPE TOMATOES
2 pints

STRIP STEAK
2 1½-in.-thick (about 12 oz each)

WHITE WINE VINEGAR
2 Tbsp

RED ONION
½ small, finely chopped

1. Heat oven to 450°F. Toss green beans and tomatoes with **2 Tbsp olive oil** and a **pinch each kosher salt and pepper** on a large rimmed baking sheet. Roast until vegetables begin to brown, 10 to 12 min.

2. Meanwhile, heat **2 tsp oil** in a large cast-iron skillet on medium. Season each strip steak with ¼ tsp each salt and pepper and cook until browned, 3 min. per side. Transfer skillet to oven and continue roasting strip steaks to desired doneness, 3 to 4 min. for medium-rare. Transfer strip steaks to cutting board and let rest at least 5 min. before slicing.

3. In bowl, combine white wine vinegar, **2 Tbsp oil** and ¼ tsp each salt and pepper; stir in onions. Serve sliced steak with vegetables and spoon vinegar-onion mixture on top.

SERVES 4 *About 480 cal, 29.5 g fat (8 g sat), 40 g pro, 480 mg sodium, 14 g carb, 5 g fiber*

BONUS IDEA	**Leftover Lunch:** *Toss any leftover vinegar-onion mixture with ½ cup canned white beans (rinsed) in a large bowl. Then toss with any leftover steak, tomatoes and green beans and 3 cups mixed greens.*

Jammy Grilled Cheese

ACTIVE **20 MIN.** | TOTAL **20 MIN.**

INGREDIENTS

SOURDOUGH BREAD
8 slices

JAM
1/2 cup (any flavor)

BRIE
8 oz, cut into 8 slices
with rind intact

ARUGULA
2 heads, thick
stems discarded

**LEMON
VINAIGRETTE**
3 to 4 Tbsp

1. Spread 1/2 Tbsp softened unsalted butter on one side of each slice of sourdough bread (**4 Tbsp softened unsalted butter** total). Spread 2 Tbsp jam on unbuttered sides of 4 slices sourdough bread, then top each with 2 slices Brie. Top with remaining sourdough bread slices, butter sides up.

2. Heat large skillet on medium-low. Add 2 sandwiches and cook until bread is golden brown and cheese melts, 2 to 3 min. per side. Repeat with remaining sandwiches.

3. In large bowl, toss arugula with 3 Tbsp lemon vinaigrette adding an additional Tbsp if necessary to fully coat. Serve with grilled cheese.

SERVES 4 *About 690 cal, 34 g fat (18 g sat), 22 g pro, 985 mg sodium, 75 g carb, 3 g fiber*

Roasted Sausage and Grapes with Polenta

ACTIVE **20 MIN.** | TOTAL **25 MIN.**

INGREDIENTS

SWEET ITALIAN SAUSAGE
6 small links (about 1½ lbs)

SHALLOTS
4 small, cut into 1-in.-thick wedges

RED GRAPES
1½ lbs seedless, snipped into small bunches

FRESH ROSEMARY
2 heaping Tbsp

INSTANT POLENTA
1 cup

1. Place large rimmed baking sheet in oven and heat oven to 450°F. Rub Italian sausage links with **½ Tbsp olive oil**, carefully place on heated pan and roast 6 min.

2. Move Italian sausage to one side of pan; on other side, toss grapes, shallots and rosemary with **2 Tbsp oil** and **¼ tsp each kosher salt and pepper**. Turn Italian sausage and nestle among grapes, then roast until Italian sausage is cooked through and grapes are beginning to burst, 12 to 15 min. more.

3. Meanwhile, cook polenta per pkg. directions; stir in **1 Tbsp oil**. Slice Italian sausage. Serve polenta topped with sliced sausage, grapes and shallots along with any pan juices.

SERVES 4 *About 711 cal, 38 g fat (11.5 g sat), 27 g pro, 780 mg sodium, 65 g carb, 3 g fiber*

BONUS IDEA	**Next-Day Breakfast:** *Have extra grapes? Roast them with a little olive oil (no herbs), then toss with maple syrup. After they cool slightly, pile them onto Greek yogurt with toasted nuts or granola.*

Cauliflower Alfredo

ACTIVE 25 MIN. | TOTAL 25 MIN.

INGREDIENTS

FETTUCCINE
12 oz

CAULIFLOWER
8 oz, thinly sliced

GARLIC
1 clove, sliced

YELLOW ONION
1/2 small, thinly sliced

NUTRITIONAL YEAST
1 Tbsp

1. Cook fettuccine per pkg. directions. Drain pasta and return to pot.

2. Heat **1 Tbsp olive oil** in a large skillet on medium. Add cauliflower, garlic and onion and cook, covered, until just tender, 5 to 7 min. Add **2 cups water** and simmer until vegetables are very soft soft, 3 to 5 min. Drain, reserving cooking liquid.

3. Transfer vegetables to blender along with nutritional yeast and **½ tsp kosher salt** and puree, adding just enough reserved vegetable liquid to get blender moving (about ¼ cup), until smooth. Toss with fettuccine, adding some vegetable liquid if pasta seems dry, and sprinkle with **pepper**.

SERVES 4 *About 370 cal, 5.5 g fat (1 g sat), 13 g pro, 250 mg sodium, 67 g carb, 5 g fiber*

Bacon, Egg and Cheese Stackers

ACTIVE **35 MIN.** | TOTAL **35 MIN.**

INGREDIENTS

BACON
4 slices

HASH BROWN PATTIES
2

EGGS
4 large

FLOUR TORTILLAS
4 8-in.

EXTRA-SHARP CHEDDAR
¼ cup coarsely grated

1. Cook bacon in a large skillet on medium heat until crisp, 5 to 6 min.; break into pieces. Cook hash brown patties per pkg. directions, then halve crosswise. Wipe out skillet and heat **1 Tbsp olive oil** on medium. In bowl, beat eggs with **¼ tsp each kosher salt and pepper**. Add to skillet and cook, stirring with rubber spatula every few seconds, to desired doneness, 2 to 3 min. for soft-scrambled eggs; set aside.

2. Place flour tortillas on cutting board, then place 1 piece hash brown in center of each. Dividing evenly, top hash browns with bacon, eggs and extra-sharp Cheddar (about 1 Tbsp each). Tightly wrap tortilla around filling, pleating edges, then place pleated side down.

3. Heat **1 tsp oil** in a large nonstick skillet on medium. Place 2 wraps, pleated sides down, in skillet and cook, pressing down on each wrap and standing up on sides as necessary, until entire tortilla is golden brown, about 2 min. per large sides and 1 min. for smaller sides. Repeat with remaining wraps. Cut wraps in half. Drizzle with **hot sauce** for a quick hit of heat and serve with **salad** if desired.

SERVES 4 *About 476 cal, 30 g fat (7 g sat), 15 g pro, 636 mg sodium, 38 g carb, 2 g fiber*

WEEK 10 DINNERS
Week-At-A-Glance

DAY 64
Seared Scallops and
Escarole Salad

DAY 65
Sheet Pan Roasted Chicken

DAY 66
Five Spice Steak and Broccoli

DAY 67
Aleppo Pork Chops
with Potatoes and Greens

DAY 68
Pierogi with Sauteed Cabbage

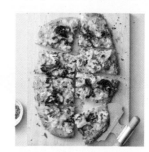

DAY 69
Roasted Cauliflower Pizza

DAY 70
Everything Bagel Bake

NOTES

_____

_____

_____

_____

_____

WEEK 10
Shopping List

PRODUCE
1   yellow onion
3   small red onions
1½ lbs small Yukon gold potatoes
1   small acorn squash
1¼ lbs broccoli
½   medium head cauliflower
    (about 1 lb)
½   small savoy cabbage
    (about 1 lb)
1   bulb fennel
2   12-oz pkgs. grape tomatoes
1   bunch escarole
½   cup flat-leaf parsley
1   bunch Swiss chard

MEAT & SEAFOOD
1   lb sirloin steak
2   small bone-in chicken breasts
    (about 1½ lbs total)
4   small bone-in pork chops
    (2½ lbs total)
4   slices bacon
1   lb large sea scallops

REFRIGERATED & DAIRY
6   large eggs
1½ cups whole milk
½   cup scallion cream cheese
4   oz Gruyère
1   lb pizza dough
3   Tbsp pesto

FROZEN
1   16-oz pkg. frozen potato and
    onion pierogi

BREAD & BAKERY
3   medium everything bagels

PANTRY
1   cup long-grain white rice
1   tsp Chinese five-spice powder
2   Tbsp capers
1   Tbsp black bean garlic sauce
    (we used Lee Kum Kee)
1   Tbsp maple syrup
1½ tsp Aleppo powder

COOKING STAPLES
5   Tbsp unsalted butter
2   Tbsp canola oil
1   8-oz bottle olive oil
½   tsp flaky salt
    Kosher salt and black pepper

BOOST IT

Some recipes this week
may call for these flavor
boosters and we highly
recommend sprinkling
them in if you already
have them on hand. If
you don't, it's OK—all
the recipes are great on
their own!

- Crushed red pepper
- Sesame seeds
- Scallions

Seared Scallops and Escarole Salad

ACTIVE 25 MIN. | **TOTAL 25 MIN.**

INGREDIENTS

CAPERS
2 Tbsp, rinsed and patted
dry, divided

PESTO
3 Tbsp, refrigerated

LEMONS
2

ESCAROLE
1 bunch, trimmed,
cleaned and torn into
pieces (about 10 cups)

SEA SCALLOPS
1 lb large, patted very dry

1. Chop 1 Tbsp capers and place in large bowl. Add pesto, 1 tsp lemon zest, 3 Tbsp lemon juice and **1½ Tbsp olive oil** and mix to combine.

2. Add escarole to dressing and toss to combine.

3. Heat large skillet on medium-high. Season sea scallops with **½ tsp each kosher salt and pepper**. Add 1 Tbsp oil to skillet, then sea scallops and cook until golden brown and opaque throughout, 2 to 3 min. per side. Transfer sea scallops to plates. Lower heat to medium.

4. Add remaining 1 Tbsp whole capers to skillet and cook, tossing, until crisp, about 2 min. Remove skillet from heat and add 2 Tbsp lemon juice, scraping up any brown bits. Then add **1 Tbsp cold unsalted butter** and swirl pan to incorporate. Spoon sauce over scallops and serve with escarole salad.

SERVES 4 *About 252 cal, 17 g fat (4 g sat), 16 g pro, 886 mg sodium, 9 g carb, 1 g fiber*

BONUS IDEA	**Leftover Lunch:** *A sprinkle of briny capers adds big flavor to a homemade vinaigrette—perfect for drizzling over greens. In medium bowl, combine 1 shallot (finely chopped), 2 tsp lemon zest, 2 Tbsp lemon juice, 1/4 cup parsley (finely chopped), 2 Tbsp capers (drained and finely chopped), 1 small clove garlic (grated), and 1/4 tsp each kosher salt and pepper, then gradually whisk in 1/4 cup olive oil. Drizzle over roasted vegetables or toss with greens.*

Sheet Pan Roasted Chicken

ACTIVE **25 MIN.** | TOTAL **45 MIN.**

INGREDIENTS

RED ONIONS
2 small, cut into ½-in.-
thick wedges

ACORN SQUASH
1 small (about 1 lb), cut
into ¾-in.-thick wedges

FENNEL
1 bulb, cut into ½-in.-
thick wedges

CHICKEN BREASTS
2 small bone-in (about
1½ lbs total)

THYME
8 sprigs, broken
into pieces

1. Heat oven to 425°F. Toss red onions, acorn squash and fennel with **1 Tbsp olive oil** and **¼ tsp each kosher salt and pepper** on a large rimmed baking sheet; roast 15 min.

2. Meanwhile, heat **2 tsp oil** in a medium skillet on medium. Season chicken breasts with **¼ tsp each salt and pepper** and cook, skin sides down, until deep golden brown, 8 to 10 min. Flip and cook 3 min. more. Nestle chicken breasts among vegetables on baking sheet and roast until chicken breasts are cooked through, 15 to 18 min. Transfer chicken breasts to cutting board and let rest at least 5 min. before slicing.

3. Toss vegetables with thyme and return to oven to continue roasting until ready to serve, about 5 min. Serve with chicken.

SERVES 4 *About 463 cal, 21.5 g fat (5 g sat), 33 g pro, 620 mg sodium, 38 g carb, 8 g fiber*

Five Spice Steak and Broccoli

ACTIVE 30 MIN. | TOTAL 30 MIN.

INGREDIENTS

WHITE RICE
1 cup long-grain

BROCCOLI
1¼ lbs, cut into florets,
stems peeled and sliced

SIRLOIN STEAK
1 lb, halved lengthwise
and thinly sliced
crosswise

**CHINESE FIVE-SPICE
POWDER**
1 tsp

**BLACK BEAN
GARLIC SAUCE**
1 Tbsp (we used Lee
Kum Kee)

1. Cook white rice per pkg. directions.

2. In large skillet, bring **½ cup water** to a simmer on medium. Add broccoli and cook, covered, until bright green and barely tender, 4 to 5 min. Transfer to plate; wipe out skillet.

3. In medium bowl, toss steak with Chinese five-spice powder and **½ tsp each kosher salt and pepper**. Add **1 Tbsp canola oil** to skillet and heat on medium-high. In batches, cook steak in single layer until browned, about 2 min. per side; transfer to clean bowl.

4. Reduce heat to medium and add **1 Tbsp oil**, then garlic black bean sauce and cook, stirring, until fragrant, 1 min. Add steak and any juices from bowl along with **¼ cup water**. Cook, tossing, until coated in sauce, 30 sec. Fold in broccoli. Serve over rice. Sprinkle with **sesame seeds** if desired.

SERVES 4 *About 518 cal, 23.5 g fat (6.5 g sat), 30 g pro, 479 mg sodium, 47 g carb, 3 g fiber*

Aleppo Pork Chops with Potatoes and Greens

ACTIVE **35 MIN.** | TOTAL **35 MIN.**

INGREDIENTS

PURE MAPLE SYRUP
1 Tbsp

ALEPPO PEPPER
½ tsp

YUKON GOLD POTATOES
1½ lbs small

SWISS CHARD
1 bunch (about 11 oz), stems and leaves chopped

PORK CHOPS
4 small bone-in (1¼-in. thick; about 2¼ lbs total)

1. Heat oven to 425°F. Mash together **4 Tbsp unsalted butter** (½ stick; at room temp), maple syrup, Aleppo pepper and ¼ tsp flaky salt in a medium bowl.

2. Place Yukon gold potatoes in large pot, cover with **cold water** and bring to a boil. Add **2 tsp kosher salt** and simmer until Yukon gold potatoes are tender when pierced with knife, 15 to 18 min. Using slotted spoon, transfer Yukon gold potatoes to large bowl and gently smash. Keep water simmering.

3. Add Swiss chard to simmering water; cook until just wilted, 1 to 2 min. Transfer to serving bowl with Yukon gold potatoes. Fold in 2 Tbsp Aleppo butter and **¼ tsp each salt and pepper**.

4. While Yukon gold potatoes are cooking, heat **1 Tbsp olive oil** in large cast-iron skillet on medium-high. Season pork chops with **½ tsp each salt and pepper** and cook until golden brown, 4 to 5 min. per side. Transfer skillet to oven and roast until pork chops are just cooked through, 5 to 8 min. Dividing evenly, top pork chops with remaining Aleppo butter and serve with smashed potatoes and greens.

SERVES 4 *About 603 cal, 32 g fat (14 g sat), 43 g pro, 978 mg sodium, 39 g carb, 5 g fiber*

Pierogi with Sauteed Cabbage

ACTIVE 20 MIN. | TOTAL 20 MIN.

INGREDIENTS

PIEROGI
1 16-oz pkg. frozen potato
and onion

BACON
4 slices

YELLOW ONION
1, sliced

SAVOY CABBAGE
½ small (about 1 lb),
cored and thinly sliced

**WHOLE-GRAIN
MUSTARD**
1½ Tbsp

1. Pan-fry frozen potato and onion pierogi per pkg. directions.

2. Meanwhile, cook bacon in large skillet on medium, flipping once, until crisp, 5 to 6 min. Transfer to paper towel-lined plate; let cool, then break into pieces.

3. Wipe out skillet and heat **1 Tbsp olive oil** on medium. Add onion and cook, covered, stirring occasionally, 5 min.

4. Add cabbage to onion in skillet and season with **¼ tsp each kosher salt and pepper**. Cook, covered, stirring occasionally, until vegetables are just tender, 2 to 3 min.

5. Stir in whole-grain mustard and **1 Tbsp water** and cook 1 min. Fold in bacon and serve with pierogi.

SERVES 4 *About 305 cal, 12 g fat (2 g sat), 10 g pro, 756 mg sodium, 41 g carb, 5 g fiber*

BONUS IDEA	**Leftover Lunch:** *Extra savoy cabbage leaves are a great sub for bread or wraps. Blanch leaves until just tender, about 1 min. Drain and pat dry, then fill leaves with gochujang-glazed shrimp, cucumbers and scallions, or whatever you're craving.*

Roasted Cauliflower Pizza

ACTIVE **15 MIN.** | TOTAL **40 MIN.**

INGREDIENTS

PIZZA DOUGH
1 lb

CAULIFLOWER
½ medium head (about
1 lb), thinly sliced

RED ONION
1 small, thinly sliced

FLAT-LEAF PARSLEY
½ cup

GRUYÈRE
4 oz, coarsely grated
(about 1¾ cups)

1. Heat oven to 425°F. Line a large rimmed baking sheet with parchment. Shape pizza dough into 16-in. oval and place on prepared sheet.

2. Toss cauliflower and onion with **2 Tbsp olive oil** and **½ tsp kosher salt** in a large bowl.

3. Fold parsley and Gruyère into vegetable mixture and scatter over pizza dough. Bake pizza until cauliflower is tender and crust is golden brown and crisp, 20 to 25 min. For a li'l kick, toss **¼ tsp crushed red pepper** into the vegetable mixture before topping dough if desired.

SERVES 4 *About 337 cal, 16 g fat (6 g sat), 15 g pro, 741 mg sodium, 32 g carb, 1.5 g fiber*

Everything Bagel Bake

ACTIVE **15 MIN.** | TOTAL **1 HR. 10 MIN.**

INGREDIENTS

GRAPE TOMATOES
2 12-oz pkgs.

**EVERYTHING
BAGELS**
3 medium, split and cut
into 1½-in. pieces

EGGS
6 large

WHOLE MILK
1½ cups

**SCALLION CREAM
CHEESE**
½ cup

1. Heat oven to 400°F. Toss grape tomatoes with **2 Tbsp olive oil, ½ tsp kosher salt and ¼ tsp pepper** on a small rimmed baking sheet. Roast until bursting and beginning to reduce, 25 to 30 min.

2. On large rimmed baking sheet, arrange everything bagels and toast in oven with tomatoes until lightly golden brown, 8 to 10 min.

3. Meanwhile, brush a shallow 2 ½- to 3-qt baking dish with oil. In large bowl, whisk together eggs, milk and **½ tsp each salt and pepper.** Toss with toasted everything bagels; let sit, tossing occasionally, at least 15 min. and up to overnight.

4. Reduce oven 350°F. Fold tomatoes into bagel mixture, transfer to prepared baking dish and dot with cream cheese. Bake until set and knife inserted into center comes out clean, 40 to 45 min. Scatter **sliced scallions** on top if desired.

SERVES 6 to 8 *About 398 cal, 18.5 g fat (7 g sat), 16 g pro, 967 mg sodium, 42 g carb, 3 g fiber*

BONUS IDEA	**Snack Hack:** *Spread extra scallion cream cheese on crackers or bagel chips and top with smoked salmon pieces or trout roe.*

Recipe Finder

Ready to create your own meal plans? Whether you are looking for recipes based on ingredients you love or aiming to use up items you have on hand before they expire, this list will help you build weekly menus you and your family will enjoy. Happy cooking!

PRODUCE

Acorn squash

Sheet Pan Roasted Chicken, p.176

Artichokes

Artichokes (canned halves)
Seared Chicken with Cheesy Spinach and Artichokes, p.64

Artichokes (marinated)
Grilled Lamb and Artichoke Kebabs, p.132

Arugula (baby)

Grilled Lamb and Artichoke Kebabs, p.132

Sausage Sheet Pan Dinner, p.66

Asparagus

Sheet Pan Asparagus Frittata, p.102

Shrimp and Asparagus Stir-Fry, p.84

Basil

Balsamic Chicken Caprese, p.142

Creamy Corn Pasta, p.136

Shrimp and Sweet Corn "Grits", p.150

Steak with Farro Salad and Grilled Green Beans, p.118

Broccoli

Five Spice Steak and Broccoli, p.178

Pan-Fried Chicken with Lemony Roasted Broccoli, p.46

Sheet Pan Salmon, Broccoli and Rice, p.62

Brussels sprouts

Ravioli with Turkey Sausage and Brussels Sprouts, p.50

Roasted Cherry Chicken with Parmesan Brussels Sprouts, p.160

Butternut squash

Roasted Butternut Squash and Pork Chops with Cider Pan Sauce, p.32

Cabbage

Coleslaw mix
Barbecue Pulled Jackfruit Sandwiches, p.74

Red cabbage
Roasted Butternut Squash and Pork Chops with Cider Pan Sauce, p.32

Savoy cabbage
Pierogi with Sauteed Cabbage, p.182

Carrots

Steak with Harissa Butter Carrots, p.82

Cauliflower

Roasted Cauliflower Pizza, p.184

Cauliflower Alfredo, p.168

Cherries

Dried cherries
Roasted Cherry Chicken with Parmesan Brussels Sprouts, p.160

Fresh cherries
Seared Pork Chops with Cherries and Spinach, p.98

Chives

Pea and Ricotta Omelets, p.72

Corn (ears)

Creamy Corn Pasta, p.136

Grilled Pork with Smoky Corn Salad, p.128

Shrimp and Sweet Corn "Grits", p.150

Sticky Grilled Chicken with Corn and Potatoes, p.114

Escarole

Seared Scallops and Escarole Salad, p.174

Pierogi (frozen potato and onion)

Pierogi with Sauteed
Cabbage, p.182

Waffles (frozen buttermilk)

Waffle Nachos, p.116

PANTRY

Adobo sauce

Sheet Pan Chicken
Fajitas, p.126

Aleppo pepper

Aleppo Pork Chops with
Potatoes and Greens, p.180

Apple cider

Roasted Butternut Squash
and Pork Chops with Cider
Pan Sauce, p. 32

Apricot jam

Apricot Grilled Pork
Tenderloin and
Peppers, p.110

Beans

Black beans
Black Bean–Stuffed Poblano
Peppers, p.52

Butter beans
Skillet Pesto Chicken and
Beans, p.130

Cannellini beans
Tomato and White Bean
Soup, p.120

Chickpeas
Paprika Chicken with Crispy
Chickpeas and Tomatoes,
p.148

Bread

Baguette
Oil and Vinegar Chicken
Cutlet Sandwiches, p.80

Tomato Soup with Parmesan
Crostini, p.38

Everything bagels
Everything Bagel
Bake, p.186

Pitas or flatbreads
Chicken Shawarma, p.88

Rye bread
Classic Patty Melt, p.56

Sourdough bread
Jammy Grilled Cheese, p.164

Vegan brioche-style buns
Barbecue Pulled Jackfruit
Sandwiches, p.74

Capers

Seared Salmon with Charred
Green Beans, p.30

Seared Scallops and Escarole
Salad, p.174

Chicken bouillon base

Pasta e Piselli, p.42

Chicken broth

Ravioli with Turkey Sausage and
Brussels Sprouts, p.50

Chili oil

Air Fryer Salmon and Swiss
Chard, p.158

Chimichurri

Citrus-Marinated Steak and
Crispy Potatoes, p.100

Chinese five-spice powder

Five Spice Steak and
Broccoli, p.178

Chipotle mayonnaise

Grilled Pork with Smoky Corn
Salad, p.128

Coconut milk

Multicooker Coconut Beef
Curry, p.36

Coriander seeds

Steak with Harissa Butter
Carrots, p.82

Cornichons

Ham and Brie
Quesadilla, p.104

Couscous

Couscous
Cod in Parchment with
Orange-Leek Couscous, p.78

Shrimp Packets with Kale
and Couscous, p.122

Quick-cooking pearl couscous
Moroccan-Spiced Skillet
Chicken and Couscous, p.34

Cumin (ground)

Cumin-Lime Shrimp, p.134

Shakshuka, p.90

Enchilada sauce (red)

Skillet Chicken Enchiladas, p.70

Farro (quick-cooking)

Steak with Farro Salad and
Grilled Green Beans, p.118

Salsa verde

Potato and Chorizo Tacos, p.40

Sesame seeds

Sesame-Crusted Salmon with Miso-Roasted Radishes, p.144

Shawarma seasoning

Chicken Shawarma, p.88

Smoked paprika

Shrimp and Sweet Corn "Grits", p.150

Soy sauce

Kimchi and Spam Fried Rice, p.54

Sundried tomato pesto

Steak with Farro Salad and Grilled Green Beans, p.118

Teriyaki sauce

Pork, Pineapple and Onion Skewers, p.152

Sheet Pan Salmon, Broccoli and Rice, p.62

Thai red curry paste

Multicooker Coconut Beef Curry, p.36

Toasted sesame oil

Kimchi and Spam Fried Rice, p.54

Tomato paste

Moroccan-Spiced Skillet Chicken and Couscous, p.34

Tortillas

Corn tortillas
Potato and Chorizo Tacos, p.40

Skillet Chicken Enchiladas, p.70

Flour tortillas (large)
Ham and Brie Quesadilla, p.104

Flour tortillas (8-in.)
Bacon, Egg and Cheese Stackers, p.170

Vegan queso

Black Bean—Stuffed Poblano Peppers, p.52

Vegan ranch dressing

Barbecue Pulled Jackfruit Sandwiches, p.74

Vinegar

Vinegar (balsamic)
Balsamic Chicken Caprese, p.142

Vinegar (red wine)
Oil and Vinegar Chicken Cutlet Sandwiches, p.80

Vinegar (sherry)
Roasted Cod and Potatoes with Chorizo Vinaigrette, p.48

Vinegar (white wine)
Chicken à L'Orange, p.96

Apricot Grilled Pork Tenderloin and Peppers, p.110

Seared Steak with Blistered Tomatoes and Green Beans, p.162

Wine (dry white)

Linguine with Clams, p.58

Seared Chicken with Cheesy Spinach and Artichokes, p.64

Seared Pork Chops with Cherries and Spinach, p.98

BONUS CHART

	Sunday	Monday	Tuesday	Wednesday	Thursday	Friday	Saturday
Dinner Proteins							
Flavor							
Method							
Side							
Prep Notes							
Lunch							
Breakfast							
Snacks							

INGREDIENTS I HAVE:

PRODUCE:

PROTEIN:

DAIRY:

PANTRY:

GROCERY LIST:

PRODUCE:

PROTEIN:

DAIRY:

PANTRY:

BONUS CHART

	Sunday	Monday	Tuesday	Wednesday	Thursday	Friday	Saturday
Dinner Proteins							
Flavor							
Method							
Side							
Prep Notes							
Lunch							
Breakfast							
Snacks							

INGREDIENTS I HAVE:

PRODUCE:

PROTEIN:

DAIRY:

PANTRY:

GROCERY LIST:

PRODUCE:

PROTEIN:

DAIRY:

PANTRY:

64, 132 (artichokes), 116, 170 (cheddar), 176 (acorn squash); innafoto2017: 114, 128, 136, 150 (corn); Iryna: 168 (fettucine); Roman Ivaschenko: 80 (red wine vinegar); Alasdair James/E+: 184 (Gruyère); JJAVA: 52 (vegan queso); karandaev: 142 (balsamic vinegar); karina: 130, 174 (pesto); philip kinsey: 34 (tomato paste); kolesnikovserg: 32, 98, 180 (pork chops), 104 (cornichon); koosen: 54 (sesame oil); kovaleva_ka: 120, 138, 146 (zucchini); krasyuk: 38, 42, 50, 86, 106, 154, 160 (Parmesan); ksena32: 50 (cheese ravioli); kwanchaichaiudom: 164 (sourdough); Grigoriy Lukyanov: 106 (pappardelle); magraphics: 48, 66 (new potatoes); MAJGraphics: 72, 86, 90, 94, 102, 116, 170, 186 (egg); MarcoFood: 72, 112, 138 (mint); maxsol: 52 (poblano pepper), 144 (sesame seeds); Michelle: 46 (flour); Olga Miltsova: 118, 136, 142, 150 (basil); M. Makela: 68, 120, 168 (nutritional yeast); mrjpeg: 68, 112 (rigatoni); Moving Moment: 88 (pita), 90, 134 (cumin), 130 (butter beans); Max Narodenko: 126, 152 (pineapple); nata777_7: 36, 38, 66, 80, 88, 100, 110, 152, 158, 162, 176, 184 (red onion); Natika: 36, 110, 126 (red pepper), 56 (rye bread, Swiss cheese), 98 (cherries), 144 (radish); nd700: 134, 146 (cilantro); Jovan Nikolic: 158, 180 (Swiss chard); ninoninos: 52 (black beans); nito: 160 (dried cherries); nortongo: 166 (red grapes); npls: 48, 78, 94 (cod fillets); nuiiko: 36 (thai red curry paste); nungning20: 54 (kimchi); Leonid Nyshko: 96 (raw chicken); Olesia: 38, 142 (tomato); padmavathi: 70 (red enchilada sauce); olya6105: 168, 184 (cauliflower); Picture Partners: 82 (harissa), 118 (farro); Papugrat: 30, 38, 46, 52, 58, 68, 90, 120, 148, 158, 168 (garlic); Yana Perelotova: 32, 98 (whole-grain mustard); PhotoSG: 30, 62, 144, 158 (salmon); Brad Pict: 64 (garlic and herb cheese); pinkyone: 164 (lemon vinaigrette); Pixel-Shot: 62, 68, 84, 128, 132, 136, 146, 154 (scallions); Роман Фернаті: 58, 86, 184 (parsley); Alexander Raths: 82 (hanger steak); rimglow: 134 (lime); Route66Photography: 40, 70 (corn tortilla); Ryzen0827: 36 (beef chuck roast); Shakzu: 40 (russet potato); Volodymyr Shevchuk: 50 (Italian turkey sausage), 112 (Pecorino); showcake: 114 (lime juice); Serhiy Shullye: 182 (savoy cabbage); Tatyana Sidyukova: 72, 106, 138 (ricotta), 142 (mozzarella); siraphol: 82 (honey); somchaisom: 54, 62, 134, 144, 178 (white rice); Dmitri Stalnuhhin: 102 (goat cheese); Andrei Starostin: 152 (baby bell peppers); Yeti Studio: 94 (salt and vinegar potato chips); SunnyS: 82 (rainbow carrots); supamas: 30, 96, 118, 120, 130, 162 (green beans), 82 (coriander); Dmitriy Syechin: 132 (lamb leg); Timmary: 86, 150, 170, 182 (bacon); tpzijl: 78, 138 (leeks); travelbook: 158 (chili oil); uckyo: 100 (chimichurri), 118 (skirt steak); Tim UR: 34, 46, 64, 80, 126, 142, 148, 160, 176 (chicken breast); uwimages: 58, 86 (linguine); valery121283: 50, 160 (Brussels sprouts), 64, 80, 98, 102 (spinach), 176 (fennel); Viktor: 74 (vegan ranch dressing); Daniel Vincek: 70 (rotisserie chicken); vitals: 36 (coconut milk); vm2002: 116 (waffle); xamtiw: 74 (barbecue sauce); Natalya Zavyalova: 88, 130 (chicken thighs); zcy: 84, 102 (asparagus); Mara Zemgaliete: 138, 184 (pizza dough), 154 (cottage cheese); zigzagmtart: 112 (summer squash); Angelina Zinovieva: 15; Ирина Гутыряк: 148 (chickpeas).

BOOK DESIGN
Caroline Pickering

RECIPE DEVELOPMENT
Joy Cho, Susan Choung, Tina Martinez, Kate Merker

Library of Congress Cataloging-in-Publication Data is on file with the publisher.

ISBN 978-1-955710-35-0

Printed in China

2 4 6 8 10 9 7 5 3 1 hardcover

HEARST

MAKE LIFE A LITTLE EASIER
AND A LOT MORE FUN.

GET EVEN MORE OF THE GOOD STUFF!

Discover essential tools
from Good Housekeeping,
including expert-tested
products and an exclusive
membership program
that will help you open up
a world of possibilities.

Find Inspiration with *Good Housekeeping!*
GOODHOUSEKEEPING.COM/INSPIRE